beyond the shores of sun and stars

a quest into the tempest

Original photography by the author
Book design by Elena Reznikova

ISBN:
978-1-7336975-0-7 (paperback)
978-1-7336975-1-4 (hardcover)

for my family
my living sea

with depths of gratitude to all who collaborated
in creating this work through their inspirations:

my wonderful wife Deborah
for the countless iterations of reading aloud and editing
and crafting shape out of the formless

Thomas Dentici, Theophane Boyd and Joseph Boyle
three guiding stars forever together

Maureen and Michael
and the passages which thrive undisturbed, unceasing

and those named and nameless, intimate and distant,
whose unique influences mix, clash, resonate and create

Contents

Preface

I SEEK THE GIFT of the book presented here. As I begin to write it, I realize I am unable. No desire, however fervent, can give shape to an essence as overwhelming and wondrous as that here courted. Yet one guide has arrived already, and from this one I ask help. It is the gift of how to receive gifts. For all I understand at this outset is that riches come to those open to them—offerings of inspiration, imagination and creation. Such treasures may not be captured like a prize, though. They rise only when they wish to be revealed, as they are shy and wary of any who would claim them as their own.

At some odd hour and slant of light, a disorienting movement surfaced. Perhaps I was in the woods where storm winds paddled the branches in wild turns and twists. Or I may have been struck by the beauty of a flock of crows in haphazard, fractured flight. Again, it might have been when I gazed into eddies of the river and their broken scatterings at shore's edge. Wherever the occurrence, a mercurial pattern emerged. If this movement had a voice, it said: "My world is different from your world. Unpredictable, yes, but not scary. Alive in motion, uncertainty and…treasures. I will grant you proof: the gift of how to receive gifts."

I stood silent. Stray winds and crows and currents spun across my vision. Everything became confused, unknowable. The stability of each moment fled instantly with the next.

Nothing held, nor could be, yet something stirred within. Something which called to me, an innocence to which I belonged. A place free from plans or goals. Utterly beyond them. Laughable to believe that plans could be asserted on such a world. Upended I fell as into an ocean's swirling fathoms. Bewildering, yet beautiful, for to be entered into its turns is to receive the gift of how to receive gifts.

To the reader who ventures into these pages, an approach is requested: Consider traveling this book, not as on a path leading to an end, but as in a forest wandering without destination. Noticing the small; unafraid of confusion; watchful for discovery. An invitation to collaborate with this work. Together questioning our perceptions of reality and loosening their hidden assumptions. Daring to seek new eyes with which to see. Embarking into the wilds, where unimaginable treasures humbly gift themselves—not from these words, but from the strivings of your own soul.

No clear path is offered here. Yet if you are suffering in storms you do not understand, this book too suffers and enters. It travels with you in the tempest, ever-farther from what we know, ever-closer to who we are.

"Many Things are About to be Born"

—TITLE OF A POEM BY JEAN GEBSER

beyond the shores
of sun and stars

...Come, my friends,
'Tis not too late to seek a newer world.
Push off, and sitting well in order smite
The sounding furrows; for my purpose holds
To sail beyond the sunset, and the baths
Of all the western stars, until I die.
It may be that the gulfs will wash us down;
It may be we shall touch the Happy Isles,
And see the great Achilles, whom we knew.

—ALFRED, LORD TENNYSON, *ULYSSES*

A Loose Introduction

THIS TEXT STRUGGLES with language to enter a world unknown to words. How to describe, for example, a sense of
foreignness in one's own life? A gnawing homesickness for a
place beyond current reality. A haunting call in the heart toward
a lyrical land. We hear its hidden music; we feel its dance. We
sense such a world, perhaps in undulations of wind and water,
in ceaseless movements of light upon landscapes, or in other
patterns drawing us toward them. While this place is often
referred to in these pages as creation, we remain unsure what it
is. More than lyrical, its movements spiral untamed. Its music
seemingly impossible without its discordance. Contradictions
abound, and words find no firm ground. Thus, beware: there is
nothing here to know.

Let us start, perhaps, with the end. Under our current
mode of thinking, reality is viewed in terms of measurable
space and progressive time. Its order is objective in nature—a
world factual, existing separate from the viewer. An outlook
which prizes clarity and understanding. This method of reality
is becoming increasingly rigid and dysfunctional, though—
so much of the world aches for healing. Nature, meanwhile,
perceives reality differently. Teeming, nonlinear interactions
pervade. Attractions in feedback loops billow into swarming
scales, spontaneously ordering, adapting and creating anew.
Inviting us into something other than understanding, into

participation and belonging, into relationship. A new way of perceiving and living. Creation at work in us. The coming of a *healing* world. This coming is not a process of calm awakening, however. As countless human traditions teach us, beginnings strain to the surface only through difficult journeying into the unknown. We must struggle in collaboration with creation.

The journey inevitably begins with an upending of familiar safeguards. Life is out of place and we strive to make sense of it. Instead of employing outdated tools of structured thought, though, we are tasked to face the crisis differently. We question the underlying assumptions to our thoughts and perceptions. We unearth influences shaping our views. We mistrust old habits and embark on a quest toward new possibilities. A challenging crossing into uncertain lands.

By boldly facing our misperceptions of reality, the transitional phase of the journey commences. Our objective worldview departs while no new worldview arrives, so we are left to drift in ambiguity. All moves in a strange fluidity, beautiful though painful, for we grieve the loss of an understandable world. Here we are tasked to shun opinions and answers, choosing only uncertainty in the face of opposing choices. Confusion surrounds, although confusion is an acceptable alternative to hollow concepts and counter-concepts. The twisting path calls us toward something greater, something rare and real.

The journey ultimately presents a supreme trial. We are again tasked, this time to release an entire world long upheld by our perceptions. Though no higher vision is gifted, no greater dimension, for the notion of reality as dimensional is itself trapped in our existing mental outlook. The universe moves from viewable to relational. We are drawn into involvement with the living motions and patterns of a new reality. Our world comes alive. However, this writing claims no knowledge of the wonders which creation may ultimately hold. We explore here merely its workings in our lives. Its stirrings awakening the soul—rhythms we do not understand that are pulling us outward toward echoing rhythms. An attraction moving us through loss into life, through endings into beginnings.

We are dreamers of new worlds and explorers toward them, realizing the path winds inscrutably, seemingly without direction. Yet guides do appear at the most surprising times. Gifts arrive of the most unexpected nature. Knowing not from where they spring, though, this book offers only varying angles and textures. Topics are not presented as truths (or even as factual), but merely as fellow travelers. Wanderers like yourself who, humbled by the long journey, may offer aid and comfort or, more urgently, a burning quest of hope: Some great coming stirs to life. An undying promise rises. In our own personal journey, the longings of creation ignite.

How to introduce the mystery and miracle that is creation? One must do so slowly, respectfully, without any claims of knowing. But there are hints for those who wish to look. Patterns from across disparate human thought. As with flickering patches of morning light through the trees, shapes turn and adjust, fade and return. If we ponder them, recurrent shapes, although distinct, tend to reinforce essential parts of each other. Patterns within patterns form.

Hints, not of the past but of what lies ahead, of workings within our midst.

Or perhaps no patterns at all. Creation may be something unpredictably new, beyond description or even imagination. Something that can only be experienced and, once experienced, must be lived.

Patterns of Creation

Full fathom five thy father lies,
Of his bones are coral made,
Those are pearls that were his eyes,
Nothing of him that doth fade,
But doth suffer a sea-change,
Into something rich and strange.

—WILLIAM SHAKESPEARE, *THE TEMPEST*

Genesis

IN THE BEGINNING there is darkness. Emptiness. Formless and void it stands. An abyss, uncreated, unknowable. Into this black, a shattering thrust of light breaks—creation—dividing existence from non-existence. Light from dark. The two are named: the created day and its remnants night. Day surrenders to night and night to morn, the first day.

On the second day, the waters are separated, above and below, summoned into two: above, the heavens; below, the earth. The third brings division of the earth into sea and land. On the fourth the partition of light between sun and moon. The fifth day divides creatures, half to thrive in the sea and half on the

land. On the sixth, creatures are parted again by the birth of humanity, a vault laid between the human and the dominions it oversees, and each split yet again, male or female are they made. On the seventh day, all had been clearly divided, in opposite pairs rendered, and rest lays across the former void.

Once separated, the divisions begin to produce preference and, consequently, conflict. Brother against brother, as Cain, angered over the divine favor bestowed to his brother Abel, kills Abel. "Am I my brother's keeper?" he rhetorically asks. Humanity becomes enslaved in battles over who is favored and who is rejected. So God (Yahweh or Allah, each in its own tradition) rests no more. Noah is told how a great flood is to upend the world and how he, his family and pairs of each creature are to be launched upon the mighty seas in an ark. The former world will die and Noah shall drift lost upon the open waters. The journey of the ark is not a journey across the seas, however. The ark is without direction, aimlessly drifting on the vast oceans. There, in this lost world, Noah is finally bestowed a gift: a sign of guidance and encouragement. His dove returns to the ark holding a small tree branch signaling the closeness of a new world. The long wanderings end upon a shore where the garden of creation springs anew—a re-creation of the world.

Family battles over favor reignite, though. Jacob's children, jealous of their father's affections for Joseph, sell their brother Joseph into slavery. Humanity is halved between master and slave, the chosen and unchosen. So God again delivers a decree, this time to Moses. Rather than one man, an entire people are to be rescued. Moses is asked to free the Children of Israel from the tyranny of their enslavement in Egypt. Following the Ten Plagues, he leads the Israelites out of Pharaoh's cruel world across the Red Sea, which separates its water to permit entry into the desert beyond. As with Noah, the journey in the desert becomes not a crossing but a labyrinth. The Israelites wind its desolate sands for forty years. Lost they roam without direction. Within this painful journey, however, the people discover unexpected guidance and care. Manna and fowl to eat, water from rock to drink, and pillars of cloud and fire to follow. Moses, with a snake upon his staff, heals the dying. And at the end of these lost wanderings lies the Promised Land, where a covenant of reconciliation and renewal is forged.

A new decree has been issued. Rather than one people, an entire world is to be rescued. Out of opposition and conflict, creation is promised a great beginning, a land free of painful division. Yet first it must enter the flood or the desert—the disorienting labyrinth. All descends into wilderness where clarity is known no more. We must travel into the tempest, where the seed of a great rebirth sleeps.

Cosmos

ACCORDING TO THE DOMINANT SCIENTIFIC THEORY regarding the origin of the cosmos, reality initially consisted of an infinitely dense, hot vacuum. So dense and hot that the natural forces governing the universe were merged, unable to escape each other in the press of the vacuum. No particles existed. Nothing existed in terms of today's science. Scientists refer to this initial reality as the united force, for it contained all forces as one.

At some critical moment, a spontaneous eruption occurred of such magnitude that the initial epochs of the universe are each measured in exponential micro-second fractions. One became known as the inflationary epoch during which the cosmic energy began to cool. While the intensity of heat and energy remained immeasurable, the united primal force cooled sufficiently to commence a process described by physicists as symmetry breaking. Symmetry breaking occurs when a chaotic system separates (or breaks) into two or more stable states. Physicists believe the unified force initially split into strong and electroweak forces, then the electroweak force divided into electromagnetic and weak forces. In this manner three of the four fundamental forces governing the universe formed—strong force and weak force (which govern the interactions of subatomic and subnuclear particles) and electromagnetic force (which governs the relationships within and between atoms and the bonding of atoms into larger matter). Scientists disagree as to how the fourth fundamental force formed—gravity (which governs the relationships between matter and the formation of stars and galaxies)—but it too is believed to have occurred through symmetry breaking, perhaps as a third branch in the initial splitting of the united force.

Amazingly, in an astonishing paradox, this breaking process of creation simultaneously involves a unifying process. While fundamental forces divide, fundamental matter joins. Subatomic particles form into simple atoms, gravity gathers atoms into stars, the heat within dying stars fuses together more complex atoms, atoms combine into molecules and molecules into macro-molecules and into larger matter such as ice and dust. Rings of this matter orbiting the great mass of a sun collect, through gravity and collisions, into planets and moons. Each star becomes an orbiting solar system. Solar systems congregate into star clusters. Star clusters become galaxies that integrate into galaxy clusters that incorporate into super-clusters. Like a Russian nesting doll, the universe incorporates ever-smaller worlds into ever-greater ones.

This paradoxical description of creation would be mirrored in subsequent developments of the universe. On at least one favorable planet known as Earth, heavier metals sink through the sludge to form a metallic core and hot mantle, while lighter metals float toward its surface to cool and form a crust. On this crust, water condenses into great oceans. Soon after, a mixture of macro-molecules leap—miraculously it seems—into *life*. Through unknowable synergistic ordering, the macro-molecules marvelously organize into the first microorganism (likely an early version of bacteria) possessing the radically novel qualities of livingness. Among the qualities defining life is the capacity to reproduce and pass traits onto offspring. The bacterium's DNA molecule separates its doubled strands, each of which forms a new complementary strand. The duplication of DNA permits a duplication of the living cell and exponential births of life. Existence surges through both unification and division.

Later synergistic creations produce photosynthetic bacteria with light-absorbing pigments capable of converting light energy into chemical energy. Algae, then plants rise and expand. From photosynthesis, oxygen levels in the biosphere dramatically climb, giving birth to animal life. Diverse participants in local resources integrate into ecosystems where dynamic flows of nutrients and energy sustain the community. Larger biomes form, then global systems, reliant on each subsystem comprising them. A vibrant order of independence and dependence reigns.

Creation involves division into diversity while simultaneously joining into organization. Scales of reality form, each scale producing new physical laws. The laws of subatomic physics, for example, are distinctly different from the laws regulating atomic interactions. Likewise, the rules governing relationships on a molecular level vary from those on a cellular level and on every scale up through cosmology. While each stratum works independently, larger reliant systems incorporate them interdependently. Autonomous levels are participants in equally autonomous higher levels. Autonomy and reliance cooperate at every scale and between all scales. The singular is the collective, the collective the singular.

Instead of a creation where everything is progressively caused, either by natural process or by divine will, reality teems within synergistic relationships spawning spontaneous worlds and stunning wonder. A twinned universe of radical, unknowable simultaneity. Where natural and divine theories of creation combine. A reality beyond such distinctions. Beyond even the boundaries of created and uncreated, material and spiritual, science and God. For creation is both common and miraculous!

Science's account of creation celebrates new realities in constant emergence. We are not trapped in any dominant method of reality. Despite its surface appearance, our world teems in perpetual re-creation, in unsleeping genesis. Dividing while unifying; breaking while building. Ceaselessly birthing worlds both unique and shared.

Lucretius

AT THE SPARK OF CREATION, according to the ancient Roman poet Lucretius, the universe is ruled by Mars, the god of warfare. Atoms in the void fall without deviation; reality is calculable in straight, unvarying lines of cause and effect. Mars reigns over this universe because it is governed by command. An unending procession of cause to effect back to cause foretells a destiny fully determinable. Nothing varies from the universal laws. Consequently, existence is predictable and subject to manipulation. The French philosopher, Michel Serres, in his studies of Lucretius named this reality *foedera fati*—a blood contract—for the price of predictability is control.

However, in the space of time, an atom deviates from its assigned path. It moves differently than the route demanded by the causes upon it. This single act proves revolutionary to all of creation as it ignites a rippling of unpredictable bends, turns and folds. Lucretius declares this revolutionary act to be the entry of Venus, the goddess of love, who breaks the grip of absolute determinism and ushers in a new world. Serres named this new reality *foedera naturae*—a natural contract—for the gift of unpredictability is naturalness, a belonging to and participation with existence. The unending sameness of the world and of its constituent parts is shattered. Growing deviations and turbulences awaken uniqueness, inviting relationship. Lucretius' great work, *On the Nature of Things*, becomes an extended love poem to the goddess Venus, who reigns over this new natural world of attraction. Venus reigns, for Venus is love—and love is, finally, to belong and embrace.

On the Nature of Things does not end with this blessed entry, however. Lucretius tells how the unpredictable swerve of atoms incites creation for they produce joinings of atoms into countless combinations of matter. Earth, air, water and fire are formed as are the beasts, foliage and fish that inhabit them. Every facet of matter enters existence incredibly distinct from all others. Each leaf of the tree, each snowflake in the sky, each newborn arrives defiantly itself. To an outsider, the calves in the herd appear indistinguishable, all from the same mold. To a calf's mother, however, her's is a beautiful, matchless creation. In a world ruled by Venus, nothing is the same as another and every moment brings ever-new realities. Each instant becomes precious, irreplaceable. Each fragment of the world is alive in astonishing rareness.

All begins with the insignificant, the tiniest, the unmeasurable swerve of one.

This reality of Venus is celebrated in Michel Serres' works as the coming of a new type of knowledge, one not based on mental capability but on lived experience. The deviations from cause no longer permit logical understanding. Yet as individuals enter the turbulences, they uncover unique passages and create new circulations. Knowledge becomes movement and, importantly, universal for it can be experienced by everyone. Not conceived or believed but traveled. Real. A knowledge inseparable from the world. Within unpredictable environments, actions serve as communication, particularly actions attracting us toward new channels, connections and collaborations. Venus' turbulences as life-giving, as transformative.

In a similar manner, Lucretius' original work describes how the abrupt, mercurial movements of Venus surprisingly carry with them a great serenity. Lucretius likens the land of Venus to cliffs overlooking violent seas. The ships imperiled on the seas below are trapped under Mars' rule as each wave rocks the ships and the sailors frantically struggle to navigate the storm. On the cliffs above, though, the storms bring invitations into possibilities, rarities and relationships. Lucretius celebrates this land as *ataraxia*, a freedom from anxiety and distress, for one is no longer gripped in the rigid chain of cause to effect. The tempest has opened a passage from Mars' world of causal control into Venus' world of precious gifts.

Lucretius' stunning poem from antiquity carries great hope to our own world. Amazingly, the turbulences rising around us may be, not painful storms we must navigate, but the entry of something extraordinary, the coming of Venus. The breaking of the grip of cause-effect objective reality, inviting a new reality. Divine Venus, goddess most rare, wins our heart and ignites a spontaneous branching of opened wonder. We fall in love with life.

Zero-Time

IN THE WRITINGS OF EVOLUTIONIST JEAN GEBSER, the author claims that humanity's understanding of time defines its stage of consciousness—its perception of the world. From timelessness to polar revolving time to arrowed forward time, humanity has perceived the universe in vastly different ways. This theme will be explored further in this book's "Dawning Dimension" discussion, but we focus here on Gebser's belief that the next dimension in human consciousness has already arrived. Not that its full power has manifested, but its evidence stirs everywhere. We no longer live in a chronological, three-dimensional world.

Between 1,500 and 500 BCE, according to Gebser, humanity began to view time chronologically, where everything moved in well-defined sequences of cause to effect. This vision of time permitted the human mind to conceptualize three-dimensional space, resulting in amazing leaps in its understanding of existence. The world could be measured and interrelationships calculated within defined margins and forces. During its most effective period, this perception of time brought great advances in science, medicine, engineering, mathematics and numerous other technical fields. The new capabilities of directed thought allowed not only understanding but also implementation—an ability to create our own world systems. Humanity thrived within a confident ego-consciousness. Time was not viewed as a problem but as something that could be used to shape the future, to build a better world.

Beginning in 1905 with the work of Albert Einstein, this confidence in time began to erode. Time was shown to be, not objectively uniform, but variable depending on relative velocity and gravity. Max Planck soon after discovered that time does not necessarily move with consistent progression but in temporal packets—instant quantum jumps. Niels Bohr then asserted that time may simultaneously operate in two realms, a "complementarity" reality of particle and wave, both leaps and progression. Black holes introduced theories on a warping of time within their immense gravities. Certain quantum theories eliminated time altogether except as a function between two variables. Time could no longer be viewed as cleanly moving from past to present to future. Recently, technology has condensed time by shrinking space. Great distances can be reached in less and less time. Through smartphones and the internet, the speed of our computer interactions is nearly instantaneous. Not only instantaneous but also exponential as social networking disburses our communications in rapid multiplying branches.

What have these developments in time brought with them? Gebser observed back in the 1950's that humanity was already suffering from a sense of lack of time. Advances in technology were, even then, hinting at the experience of zero-time. Gebser used the term zero-time to express the experience of having no time and, to Gebser, no time means no space. This brings growing anxiety and despair. Humanity feels that it is standing at some edge, at the brink, with nowhere left to go. Breathless. Crushing. The future is thwarted, overwhelming. There is no time. There is no future. No future, and therefore no hope. The confidence of forward time seems so distant—that long-ago era of building toward a better world.

This suffering is the beginning of a new era of time, according to Gebser. Although distressing, he assures us that we are experiencing creation at work. "Anxiety is the great birthgiver," Gebser writes. It signals the dysfunction and exhaustion of one type of order and the accumulating power of a new order striving for birth. Humanity begins to experience a sense of untamed time. The walls of chronologically and spatially-conceived systems are crumbling. Time is not behaving as it should. To the contrary, it is rising up, impossible to grasp or control, bursting from its sterile usable segments. Time is rupturing the logical while ushering in something miraculous.

But what? Gebser offers a suggestion. In a reality where time is usable, we crave to make order out of chaos, to shape effects. But zero-time thwarts our efforts and anxiety overwhelms. We feel frantically at the end, without hope for a future. In such moments, Gebser advises us to realize that our despair exists only in an objectively timed world. By recognizing anxiety as a component of objective time, we need not claim an end; instead, we claim a freedom. We admit that it is impossible to effect order, to effect anything at all. So we are free of time as we have known it. We cease using time. We cease controlling the future. Zero-time dominates so we simply stop, which opens time. The jumbled disorderings we are experiencing are not chaos requiring the imposition of order. They are instead dynamic reorderings, an emerging livingness.

Our world is no longer uniformly timed or logically understood, but it may be experienced and shared. The brink allows a break-though. A new deep sense of *security*—somehow—in the "out there," out beyond conceptual words and images, beyond the walls and windows which previously framed our reality. A mysterious goodness in the unwalled movements. Participation and belonging. Thrown <u>into</u> life. Alive. A part of. A new creation.

Nonlinear Systems

IN 1961, THE INTELLECTUAL WORLD OF PHYSICS was ironically rocked by the simple numerical rounding of a meteorologist. Edward Lorentz discovered that, in rounding insignificant decimal numbers in his computerized weather simulations, vastly different forecasts were produced. This led to his theory of the "butterfly effect." It states that the tiniest difference in any measurement used to calculate a forecast will result in wildly diverging predictions over the forecast period. Turbulence as slight as that caused by a butterfly's wings will produce overwhelming weather changes within a span of days to weeks. The effect of Lorentz' theory seems counterintuitive—how could such a small event have such a large effect—yet confirms the obvious: weather forecasts multiply in error over time.

Lorentz' discovery led to a new field of study probing the workings of nonlinear systems, also known as chaos systems or open systems. Theorists found that the unpredictability of weather patterns results from the nonlinear nature of their movements. These movements are not random, however. They simply operate outside of traditional sequential order. If weather were a sequential system, the butterfly's turbulence would maintain its linear relationship with adjacent influences and provide only a minimal effect on the overall system. Nonlinear systems, on the other hand, fold inward and out without regulated position. Each small influence touches distant points of the system, and the areas so influenced fold and influence other distant regions. This pattern amplifies the original influence exponentially through the system, resulting in a radically different weather pattern. Within nonlinear systems, each minor influence provides an extraordinary effect.

These studies also revealed that nonlinear movements do not operate on the fringes of reality. Everywhere in nature we find patterns of seemingly insignificant individual behavior resulting in magnificent collective order. In a flock of birds, for example, each member is attracted to other bird movements, particularly to the flock as a whole. At the same time, each acts individually as it follows its unique instincts and preferences. Continually attracted toward the flock, a bird may also be drawn away from it as it responds to food sources, shelter and predator avoidance. This results in a nonlinear interacting flow of the flock, a collective movement known as swarm. No leader directs the flock. Instead, by simultaneously allowing conformity and uniqueness, an incredible adaptability is harnessed. The flock creatively responds to ever-changing environments through the distinct gifts of its individual participants.

This same dynamic provides organization to an ant colony. Like the bird flock, ants are free to pursue individual preferences while simultaneously following simple attraction rules. As ants walk, they leave behind a light trail of pheromones drawing others to the trail, and increased travel multiplies the trail's attraction. For example, a foraging ant may locate a food source, which invites another to the trail, which attracts two more. Travel itself multiplies travel in an exponentially building feedback loop. It is important to note that the ants are *attracted*, not obligated, to follow the trail. Any particular ant may wander off, perhaps to find another food source and begin a new feedback loop. Similarly, the ants' complex, multi-layered nest is built through rules influencing them to pick up and move previously handled grains of soil. The teeming interaction of thousands of ants pursuing unique preferences, coupled with simple attraction rules, builds amplifying organization until a fully functioning colony emerges.

Also, when a disruption in the organization occurs, such as a flood, drought or other changed condition, the colony demonstrates amazing adaptability. Through the same decentralized movements and multiplying loops, the disrupted nest adjusts and reforms in ways responsive to the conditions. Order is created out of disorder or, more accurately, order and disorder live in exchange, dynamically interacting as the order responds to a turbulent world.

As will be explored elsewhere in this book, nonlinear patterns not only cooperate in dynamic ordering but also create *new* order. On microscopic levels, volatile chemicals interplay in rising collaborative movements until they reach a critical point, springing into a molecule with completely novel properties. Within magnetic material, the random spins of electrons start to line up in parallel formations, attracting a doubling and re-doubling of the behavior until a sudden magnetic field forms. Chaotic water molecules in a boil begin to trace movements of other molecules, which attract multiplying volumes into the movements until convection currents spontaneously vault into existence. In countless examples, decentralized individual movements follow attraction loops that build to a threshold, leaping into creation. Disordered conditions jump to ordered states of incredible originality.

These studies illustrate the existence of an entirely new method of reality in our midst. We see it everywhere. The surrounding flocks and winds gift us growing trust in dramatic patterns—the motions of the ever-new. Structured linear order gives way to teeming real-time order. A closed system world moves to an opened system world. A miraculous power strives forth. An untamable essence rises and moves upon this earth. We step within, humbled in its vast, whirring goodness.

The Promise

THROUGHOUT HISTORY AND ACROSS CULTURES, a promise has echoed like a thousand rolls of thunder. A great promise— *the* promise—that in the same manner as the original void had been divided into twos, oppositions will reunite and, from this marriage, a new genesis will spring. A fulcrum upon which creation aspires.

From ancient Hebrew writings, an announcement of an imminent coming in which contradictions join and divisions heal. The infinite shall dwell in the land of the finite (Ps. 27:14). The blind will see (Is. 29:17), the desert will bloom (Is. 35:1) and the lost will be embraced like lambs to the shepherd's breast (Is. 40:11). The wolf is to graze with the lamb, the lion with the calf (Is. 11:1-10). All of humanity will see it together (Is 40:5). A new law of the holy shall govern the earth, till the moon be no more (Ps. 72:7-8).

From Chinese antiquity, we receive a teaching embodied in the yin/yang symbol. This design expresses not only how oppositions are dependent, but how each is contained in the other. To the rational mind, one pole is the antithesis of its opposite. The two exist in mutual exclusivity. How can life also be death, the negation of life? How can light be darkness, the lack of light? In the intermingling of poles reflected in the yin/yang, polarities are inexpressibly entwined, fulfilled in opposition. Like the tides of the sea, every advance carries its retreat. Every rise its fall. The abundance of day embracing, in its very abundance, the rest of night.

From scrolls found in the Egyptian pyramids containing instructions for navigating the afterlife, a message of unification. Typical is a depiction of the deceased standing in a stream cupping water in the right hand—water being a symbol of life—while holding a sail in the left hand—wind being a symbol of death. The deceased is thus instructed how death is not an end but a transformation. Life and death are not a succession of events but an interlacing. In death, expect birth.

From the first teachings of Jesus announcing the kingdom of heaven, the poor are proclaimed as blessed. This is essential, for it is the key to all that follows. The lost are found; the least are the greatest. Jesus is not the messiah of expectation. If you are to accept his promise, you must accept the contradiction in his message of rebirth. His healing is not a cleansing away of strife, but is wholeness rising from within brokenness. It is death *and* life, one incomplete without the other. A kingdom mending the division between poor and blessed, least and greatest, divine and mortal.

From other traditions, contradictions join in transformative power. Quetzalcoatl, the Aztec god of creation—of both dawn and fertility—is pictured as an earth-bound serpent coupled with a winged bird. The Incan creator of all, Viracocha, is both storm-god and sun-god, its heavenly tears the living waters of earth. Hermes, the great transformative god of Olympus, carries his caduceus staff depicting two intertwined snakes in completion—his symbol for transformation. Across so many ancient cultures, sacrificial offerings of death are made as healing for the community, as new life.

This theme of transformative power arising from a joining of opposites is reflected, of course, in nature itself. Male and female of every species couple. One widening, opening, offering; the other lengthening, accepting, taking. Together enflaming the ultimate mystery of conception. Like the double helix of DNA, opposites attach and explode in generative creation.

In this same manner, day converges with night so to birth the dawn. One polarity is active—building but exhausting itself. Its opposite is restful—declining yet renewing. Summer grows until it abounds in its harvest of ripened fruit; winter reclines until it abounds in its harvest of springtime. Winter is not dead, not a mere negation of summer. It is alive in its own miraculous workings of rebirth. Or, more truly, summer and winter are alive in each other, together forging the life-giving seasons.

This joined power is expressed too in the indefinable beauty of the moon and its synchronicity of dark and light. Holding both the clarity of day and mystery of night, the moon carries in its sway the tidal rise and fall of oceans. Similarly, folklore portrays the moon as a portal for the soul's departure from and entry into this world; that is, a threshold of both death and birth. Day within night, high within low, birth within death. Powerful reconciliations within the lovely shimmering dark-light of the moon.

A reconciliation of all of heaven and earth. At the end of time, biblical prophecy tells us, a New Jerusalem will descend from the clouds where God and humanity together dwell. In the center of this holy city stands the Tree of Life. So amazing that the Tree of Life is discussed in the Christian Bible at its beginnings in *Genesis* and at its conclusion in *Revelation*. In the first instance, humanity is barred from the Tree of Life, separated and isolated. In the last instance, both heaven and creation gather to it once more, the Tree symbolic of all-embracing union.

In each manifestation of the promise, no pole prevails over its twin. Light and life do not defeat darkness and death. We are not promised the vastness of the gods. Instead, we are promised *transformation*. The manifest in love with the boundless; the vast in devotion to the small. Oppositions fall into the other's arms, reconciled, entwined, completed. The mortal still fallen yet redeemed in embrace. Broken *and* whole. Lowly *and* immense. Not a combination, a mellowing, but a dynamic relationship, an intimate consummation. Infinity draped in the adoring arms of limitation.

New worlds are opening, but not as we might have envisioned. Our expansion awakens in our reduction, our beginning in our end.

a time of disruption,
of questioning our own perceptions,
of recognizing our own pain

The Journey Begins

All lost! to prayers, to prayers! all lost!

*This thing of darkness I
Acknowledge mine.*

—WILLIAM SHAKESPEARE, *THE TEMPEST*

Crisis and Separation

The Hero's Journey

"It is not society that is to guide and save the creative hero, but precisely the reverse. And so every one of us shares the supreme ordeal—carries the cross of the redeemer—not in the bright moments of his tribe's great victories, but in the silences of his personal despair."

—JOSEPH CAMPBELL, *THE HERO WITH A THOUSAND FACES*

THE ONLY TRUE PATTERN OF CREATION is the one lived.

In his celebrated study on mythological tales, *The Hero With a Thousand Faces*, Joseph Campbell proposes that all human cultures share a single pattern of myth: that of the hero's journey. Stories repeating in various forms across human history tell how a hero, restlessly sensing the deterioration of society, follows a call to venture outside the known boundary of his or her world. Within the strange lands beyond, the hero faces numerous challenges, endures a supreme ordeal, receives a divine gift and returns to spark a rebirth of the homeland.

What is the tenor of the initial call demanding a desperate break from the hero's known world into the wilds? It is described as a loss of something vital. A sense that the life-sustaining force of the community is dissipating, that the existing culture is exhausting itself. No longer is it able to creatively respond to crises. Static lives stand everywhere lacking vitality. Where is leadership? Where is genius? Where is human fire? The hero feels closed in a suffocating box. The existing world is profoundly amiss, while old ways respond with the same empty answers. A mysterious potency summons the soul to break from the box. An urgent voice calls to courageously take a leap. To go beyond what we name and know. To admit to a schism in our society and, as such, in ourselves. To realize that no solution exists in the whole of this world, for the idea of solution itself perpetuates the decline. The only answer to death is birth. And so it must be, and so we must go.

The hero proceeds to a threshold where s/he encounters a guardian of the passage. The guardian must be battled or appeased, whereupon the hero descends into the kingdom of the dark unknown, either alive or, if defeated in battle, in death. Having entered the world beyond, the hero travels through strange, unfamiliar lands. Various forces along the journey threaten and test the hero while others aid and guide. The prior images which shaped the hero's vision of self and reality begin to break down. What was fixed and solid melts away, opening possibilities. As Campbell notes, we enter "the ambiguities of the unconscious—thus signifying the support of our conscious personality by that other, larger system, but also the inscrutability of the guide that we are following, to the peril of all our rational ends." (Campbell, pg. 60 [New World Library third ed. 2008])

Filled with both danger and delight, the land exhibits none of the predictable laws of the known world. Fierce monsters offer guidance while kind maidens portend menace, and one may suddenly become the other. Goddesses, blind beggars, tricksters, flying snakes and every assortment of confusion abounds. With each challenge, the hero must learn to atone and forgive, to battle and conquer, or to seduce and consummate, but which and how? Direction lies hidden, only to arrive at the most unexpected hour and form:

"Once having traversed the threshold, the hero moves in a dream landscape of curiously fluid, ambiguous form, where he must survive a succession of trials. ...the beginning of the long and really perilous path of initiatory conquests and moments of illumination. Dragons have now to be slain and surprising barriers passed—again, again and again." (Campbell, pgs. 81, 90)

Eventually all paths are blocked. There is no conquering or consummating. There is no hero-like passage to navigate. There is only an ordeal that reduces the prior trials to triviality. Identities which were weakened (and arrogantly believed surpassed) are faced with a final painful dissolution. The hero is no longer asked to open to possibilities, but to surrender to inevitabilities. The ultimate threshold beyond the threshold. The hero is tasked to answer this desperate situation with the most courageous response: trust. The hero clings to loosening vines over the abyss and must let go and fall. Not in resignation but, suddenly and miraculously, in relationship. The abyss is the power sought. The beyond is the return. The hero becomes the hero by surrendering the hero. Yet the hero is not surrendered. She or he lives still, and through this test receives a transformational force for society.

Passing into and through this supreme ordeal has been characterized as a dissolution, or as ceding to death:

"The individual, through prolonged psychological disciplines, gives up completely all attachment to his personal limitations, idiosyncrasies, hopes and fears, no longer resists the self-annihilation that is prerequisite to rebirth in the realization of truth, and so becomes ripe, at last, for the great at-one-ment. His personal ambitions being totally dissolved, he no longer tries to live but willingly

relaxes to whatever may come to pass in him; he becomes,
that is to say, an anonymity. The Law lives in him with
his unreserved consent." (Campbell, pgs. 204-05)

The great ordeal, when finally surrendered to, enfolds in
embrace. Because experienced by a mortal hero, it becomes
a coupling of the mortal with the divine, the created with
the uncreated. It may be symbolized by sexual union with a
god or goddess, by a second birth of baptism through sacred
waters, by theft of a celestial boon or by any number of events
representing the coupling of earth and heaven. A confluence
of worlds. A joining. Tears of misery with tears of ecstasy. An
unknowable, humbling, life-shattering gift is released.

Having gained the hard-won boon of transformation, the
hero's journey is far from complete. Subtle and dangerous
challenges await, the first of which is a risk that no return will
even be attempted. The hero is enticed to remain in the bliss
of dissolution and not re-enter the painful world of contradiction and struggle. This too must be overcome, for while the
journey has been personal, its quest has not. The homeland
still groans for healing. The hero rises to return the new power,
but then faces a winding, circuitous course of difficult passage.
Ultimately (although never assuredly), the hero again touches
the shore from which s/he embarked so long ago.

Returned, the hero's task is still not accomplished. S/he must
somehow assimilate the gift into the dominating structures of
the homeland. The risk of defeat intensifies at this stage, for the
possibility of losing the gift despite the travails in achieving it
are real. Its power may fade in the overwhelming lure of entrenched prior patterns. The journey and its gift are suddenly
unreal, impossible to accommodate amid family and function.
As Campbell states: "The returning hero, to complete his adventure, must survive the impact of the world." (Campbell, pg. 194)

The problem is to somehow retain the otherworldly power in the face of earthly existence. The hero's spirit is drawn away from its center so to deal with the periphery—the daily crises of common life. If re-subsumed by daily living, as Campbell sadly notes: "The balance of perfection is lost, the spirit falters, and the hero falls." (Campbell, pg. 192)

What can be done? According to myth, the returning hero must be insulated from touching the homeland earth. Stories tell of heroes remaining on horseback as they travel through the land so to keep their feet from the ground, or of carpets being laid before them as they walked, or of followers carrying them lest they lose their gift. The sacred must remain ungrounded so to prevent the magical electricity from running out. Another example of this insulation is the wearing of a talisman brought from the far realm which holds the hero to the divine realization gifted. A ring on a finger or stone on a necklace is worn. The precious gift which the hero bears is thus preserved and capable of being shared with the community:

> "Sequences of events from the corners of the world will draw gradually together, and miracles of coincidence bring the inevitable to pass. The talismanic ring from the soul's encounter with its other portion in the place of recollectedness betokens that the heart was there…; it betokens too a conviction of the waking mind that the reality of the deep is not belied by that of common day. This is the sign of the hero's requirement, now, to knit together his two worlds." (Campbell, pg. 196)

In the end, with the long, difficult journey of the hero complete, the great gift bestowed and carried forth into the light sparks an awakening of all of society. Two realms unite and ignite. The hero's journey has rescued the world.

Who is the hero—or, more likely, heroes—called to reju-
venate this exhausted homeland? It is anyone who accepts "a
destiny that has been summoned into life." (Campbell, pg. 196)

We listen to distant winds and waters. Is a destiny beckon-
ing in its echoes?

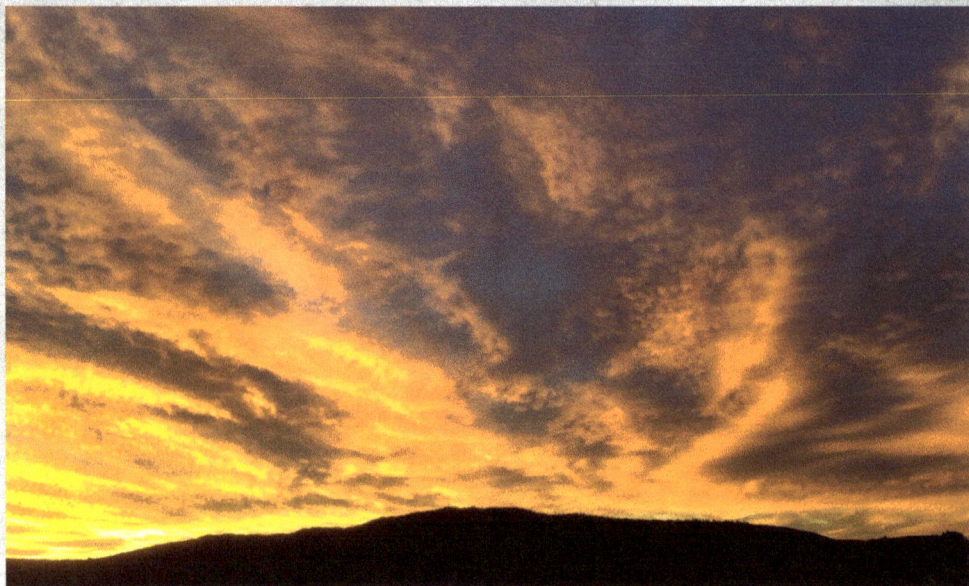

Genius and the Questioning of Perception

"Talent is like the marksman who hits a target which others cannot reach; genius is like the marksman who hits a target...which others cannot even see."

—ARTHUR SCHOPENHAUER,
THE WORLD AS WILL AND REPRESENTATION

THE FIRST STEP toward a beginning is recognizing an end. While numerous opinions exist on the exact nature of genius, a predominant view holds that genius possesses the unique ability to question the prevailing laws and assumptions of reality. Geniuses are pioneers who loosen the perceived truths claimed by their society so to envision new patterns and possibilities. The nature of this questioning lies far deeper than a mere questioning of authority, though. The tenets that must be unearthed and examined lie hidden in one's very consciousness of reality. Past geniuses amazingly find no barriers in opposites, incompatibilities or irrationalities. They move within these confusing spheres pondering and waiting for...what? Inspiration? Yes, of course, but something more. Something genuine to rise out of the confusion. They sense a falseness in dominant truths and hold to a faith in some yet-undiscovered "unreality." From this viewpoint, a genius is more akin to shaman than scientist, trusting to a happenstance gift the universe will surely one day bestow.

Some of the first geniuses recognized by history arose from a cultural period known as the Greek Awakening. During this time in ancient Greece, the authority of existing knowledge was open to question. It was a period of intense probing of the status quo, as though anything generally accepted was deemed a threat to true knowledge and art, for accepted meant rigid. Out of this awakening through its myriad geniuses, Greece invented the modern world, including the development of democracy (Cleisthenes), mathematics (Pythagoras and Euclid), philosophy (Socrates, Plato, Aristotle), the scientific method (Aristotle, Epicurus), drama (Sophocles, Euripides and Aristophanes), history (Herodotus), literature (Homer and Hesiod), sports (the Olympic Games) and architecture/sculpture (the Parthenon). Literally, a reinvention of reality.

Conversely, the next recognized group of geniuses arose during a period of intense rigidity. The entrenched European worldview held that a perfect God was enthroned in a faultless celestial heaven overlooking an imperfect, though central, earth. Heaven was viewed as a physical reality of established spheres extending upward from the flat earth. Nine separate zones increased in perfection as they moved higher toward the unblemished height of heaven. Because the heavens existed in perfection, their laws were assumed to be distinctly different from earth's laws. The sun, moon and stars were set forever in their proper place and moved across the sky in perfect circles.

In the face of searing persecution for questioning this reality, Copernicus, Galileo, Newton and others exposed the hidden assumptions of this perfection paradigm and their frail underpinnings. The heavens did not revolve above a flat earth in perfect circles, they claimed. Rather, a round earth orbited the sun as did other celestial bodies, and these heavenly rotations were not in perfect circles but in imperfect elliptical paths. Static forms did not dominate reality but, instead, constant motion. And perhaps most damaging to the perfection worldview, the same forces governing earth (such as gravity and inertia) moved the cosmos above. All of reality, whether on earth or in the heavens, could be defined by measurable masses and forces. Classical thinking was born, and a new worldview of causes, effects, components and forces emerged.

The modern genius, *par excellence*, is of course Albert Einstein, who pointed the light of scrutiny on classical thinking in the same manner his predecessors had questioned the perfection paradigm. In the year 1905, the young physicist published a paper that turned the scientific world on a tilted edge from which it has never rebalanced. The paper exposed as false one of the most basic assumptions of human knowledge—that time and space are uniform; that is, they can be measured objectively in minutes and meters. This had been the accepted assumption of reality, but Einstein refused to blindly hold to hidden assumptions. His theory defied all history of human knowledge but amazingly answered the most complex scientific questions of his time. As with most sweeping answers, its substance was simple.

A succinct description of Einstein's special relativity theory is that no simultaneous time events occur in nature. There is no one clock that can declare if two events have happened at the same time. A basic illustration involving an automobile and lightning strikes helps explain the theory, but it must be remembered that the car discussed in this example is traveling at extraordinary speeds. Let us assume that a person (who we will refer to as #1) is standing on the shoulder of a highway while another person (#2) is riding in a car down the highway away from #1 and that two lightning strikes flash from opposite directions.

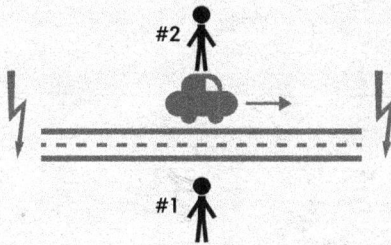

From the drawing above, it is easy to see that #1 will observe the two lightning strikes as simultaneous events as the two strikes have hit equal distances apart from #1. However, #2 is quickly heading down the road and will be in a much different position from #1 when the two strikes are observed. As you can see from the drawing below, the lightning strike to our right will be observed by #2 first and the light from the left will arrive later, for the strike on the left has farther to travel. The two lightning strikes will not be experienced as simultaneous by #2 and, in fact, will be observed at completely different times than when #1 observes them.

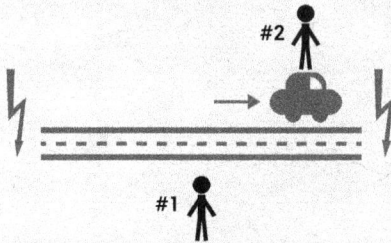

On earth where slow relative speeds exist, we can say that both strikes occurred at 9:02 p.m., for example, regardless of when observed. However, in outer space where everything is in motion at high relative speeds between objects, Einstein concluded that there exists no unmoving platform on which an objective clock can sit. All events occur when subjectively encountered. There is no absolute measure of time; no single clock governs reality.

His conclusions did not stop there. Einstein queried further: in what manner are their clocks different? Another illustration helps explain. If #1 is holding two mirrors vertically perpendicular to each other (one on the ground and one above facing it), a beam of light would reflect back and forth between the two mirrors in a vertical line. This would also be true for two mirrors held by #2, provided that #2 is traveling at a constant rate of speed, for we know from experience that someone traveling at a constant speed experiences the same reality as someone at rest (for example, a ball can be tossed straight up in a consistently moving car and it will return straight down). However, from the viewpoint of #1, the light traveling between #2's mirrors will not be vertical. Between the time that the light bounces off the bottom mirror and reaches the top mirror, the car will have moved. The line of light will be slanted from #1's perspective and, consequently, will take longer to reach the upper mirror (as the speed of light always remains constant). For #1, time has slowed down in #2's car. Of course, to #2, the reflecting beam of light is still a vertical line so its personal clock remains unchanged. But *relative to each other*, time for #2 moves more slowly. Einstein theorized that all objects in space possess different time clocks relative to each other reflecting their high-speed relative motions.

Einstein then posited a final important component to his relativity theory. Not everything is relative. The measures of

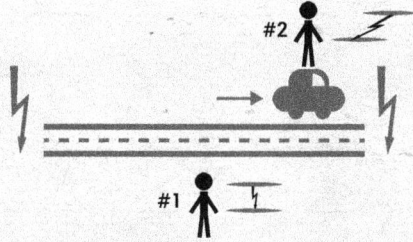

time and space may vary between observers, but time relative to space holds to an inviolable relationship. As time slows down (the measure of a minute lengthens), the measure of distance contracts so that the distance traveled by an object in motion during the "longer" minute is farther. A fixed proportionality between time and distance cannot be altered. Applying this idea to our illustrations above, while the slanted light beam in #2's car takes longer to reach the upper mirror from #1's perspective (so time is slower for #2), the mirrors are farther apart from #1's perspective, so the light reaches the upper mirror in the same amount of time, proportionally, as for # 1. Spatial measurements adjust so the relationship between time and space remains constant. The slower the clock, the shorter the measure of distance. Einstein began to refer to space and time not as separate components of reality but as one united phenomenon—spacetime.

This last observation by Einstein may be his most interesting for it raises questions as to Einstein's own hidden assumptions. He seems to have ignored the full implications of his spacetime proportionality in his thought experiments. If time and space truly enjoy exact proportionality, why did Professor Einstein conclude that only time simultaneity does not exist? His proportionality conclusion implies at least a possibility of inverse proportionality; that is, that no "same place" events occur. Yet this would be impossible, would run utterly counter to our most basic assumption of reality. Reality could not exist without objective places for events to occur.

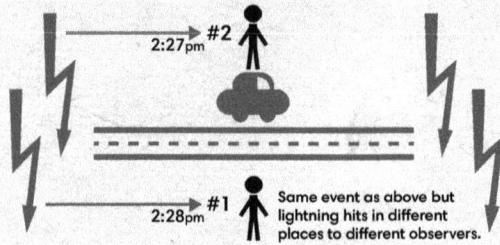

Same event as above but lightning hits in different places to different observers.

Let us return to Einstein's thought experiments. Einstein *assumed* that #1 and #2 held different relative positions due to #2's travel and, consequently, that the time of events for these two observers varied. But given Einstein's spacetime coupling, this is not the only reality possible. Alternatively, #2's clock may be quickly separating from #1's clock while their positions remain mostly unchanged. At the time that #1 observes what it views as simultaneous lightning strikes, #2 would be in a similar position as #1 *but at an earlier time* (its clock is slower). In this alternative universe, #2 would also observe simultaneous lightning strikes (or nearly so) *but they would strike in different places than they would for #1.* For there to be simultaneous lightning strikes for both #1 and #2, who would view them at two different times from the same place, the lightning would need to have hit in different places for each observer. From #2's perspective, the strikes hit closer, because #2 observes them before #1. Position becomes the relative variable in this world, not time. It is the same set of facts but with the simultaneity of time holding true while position (space) varies depending on a particular observer's relative clock.

The implication of this spacetime proportionality is an alternative world where time could be traveled in a three-dimensional time realm. Space would be sequential. It would be forward space, not time, that separates events. Rather than being able to travel to different places, to a different "here," we would be able to travel to different clocks, to a different "now."

A reversal world. Or we may exist in some mixture of these two realities. Or a possible oscillation between. A place of reversing and relative spacetime/timespace and, therefore, of measure and, therefore, of worlds.

None of this makes sense, of course, in the real world. As human genius teaches us, though, it is not about making sense. It is about questioning and doubting our sense. It is about awakening our perceptions to something startlingly new. A new real.

Artificial Truth

From where do epiphanies spring? From the fresh apple of the Tree of Knowledge bursting with first sight? From radiant star-showered skies suddenly illuminating the unseen? Or do epiphanies spring instead from disillusionment, from discontent? From loss.

So much suffering in our world is grief. The loss of love or a loved one. The loss of hopes or dreams or meaning. Where did they go? As with a departed loved one, we are not certain. We know too well only the ragged hole their loss has torn in our heart.

Sometimes the grief gets all jumbled into one. Dreams, meaning, love—is there a difference? Something deep is simply lost. There is a sense of falseness to life. What does it matter if we rise from bed this morning? Read the monotonous mountain of messages? Meet the frantic demands on our list? Why? Everything—every facet of life—spills out like meaningless junk. Nothing holds true or offers goodness. Nothing is as it seems. The racing world appears empty, senseless, devoid of meaning.

At times, we may feel this same senselessness being suffered collectively around us. Every value claiming goodness seems co-opted, manipulated toward some unseen motive. Every ideal appears tied to a calculated end. How is it that even our deepest values of compassion or freedom or honor appear on our television screens and leave us feeling ever-more hollowed? Where is the genuine? Something essential has been lost, and its absence aches and swells.

Perhaps, enlightenment involves no sudden clarity, no insight into impermanence and eternity. Could it instead reflect a moment of crisis? Might it involve that moment when nothing makes sense or, wherever it might make sense, just doesn't matter? What would such a moment offer?

It could offer a glimpse into something hidden. As the world's mechanisms become increasingly empty, our own genuineness may also be questioned. Something is not right. It is as though our truths are afraid of some discovery, of being revealed as less than true. Not wrong necessarily; more like half-truths hiding a hollowness within. We sense insincerity within our objective ideas and beliefs, a lack of something essential. As with the television, our personal views support an empty, mechanical world seemingly at odds with our living nature. In such a moment, the power of thought itself is questioned. Everything regarding the me I know as me—the very eyes with which I see—is rendered untrustworthy. So stereotyped, co-opted, false. Our logical perception of the world no longer works, or matters.

What then becomes truth? What is real?

What is the difference between far and near? The answer is simply far minus near. What is the difference between summer and winter? Strangely, we realize how difference can be extracted only in a linear world. Summer and winter are not linear—they fold into and out of each other in a surreal admixture that is not surreal at all but is purely the lack of mental. Genuinely real, but cannot be understood. Something instead that we are starved for. Something that feels deep but is instead merely real as against the mental world we claim as real. A hurting and a healing all in one, because the healing is tied to the hurting. Turning with it. Arising from it. Upheaval, yet with a longing to stay on its bewildering path, for it holds an authenticity missing from logical knowledge.

This coupling of disarray and genuineness may be compared to a run in the mountains. A lengthy brutal incline challenges the resolve of body and spirit. A terrible feeling rises of breaking down. Everything is pain: the disharmonic flux of patternless breath and heartbeat and muscles straining, the haphazard mix of resolve and defeat, of determination and desertion. The screaming temptation, and so often the decision, is to quit. This is not challenge; it is torture. It is wrong somehow, against all notions of the confidence and ease happiness entails. If we continue, however, if we allow the breakdown, the runner at some unknown point enters a place where the body synchronizes. A pace is gifted. It is not a conquering but is truly a gift, a type of harmony that cannot be conjured. Breath and heartbeat and muscle-use tie themselves to each other, but a different kind of communion also rises. The world itself becomes a dynamic component. The patterned exchange of breath draws one outward into the environment and its living involvement with the runner. Our pores open; body and spirit exchange with outer elements. A deep sense of existence emerges, a part of something greater. The individual is not obliterated. Far from it. The runner is simply cleared of structured separation and comes vitally alive in a moving interaction with life.

We suddenly look around. How is it that the mountain came to be so entwined with us and we with it? Why do we feel so vibrantly alive? So at home in the contrary winds? We know not why, and we pray to have no objective insight into it. The insight, the knowing, will kill it. There is only the knowing in the deepest recesses of the marrow of our bones. This is where we resolve to live.

Epiphanies may be sudden and marked, offering deep perspectives to new living, but no epiphany is gifted without its price. An imaginative leap requires a depth of struggle that precedes it. As with the ancient patterns of religion and myth, of tragedy and philosophy, of every lasting human tradition, we are invited on a voyage loosening the logical bonds of this world. A venture beneath the glare of day, beyond the predictable forward orbits of sun and *stars. There we are to wander on aimless seas unto an unknown shore of beginnings.*

This is the journey here failingly offered. These words and images are not the joy, but more so the work; not the fruit but the struggle. No one can predict when or if fruit will be gifted, but we know that fruit is impossible without the seed and the striving. We are trapped in a current world of great suffering and conflict. It is not too late, though; in truth it is time. It is time to awake, dear heart, awake and begin the epiphaneia; the turns and reversals which loosen and gift and, with grace, strikingly unveil the real.

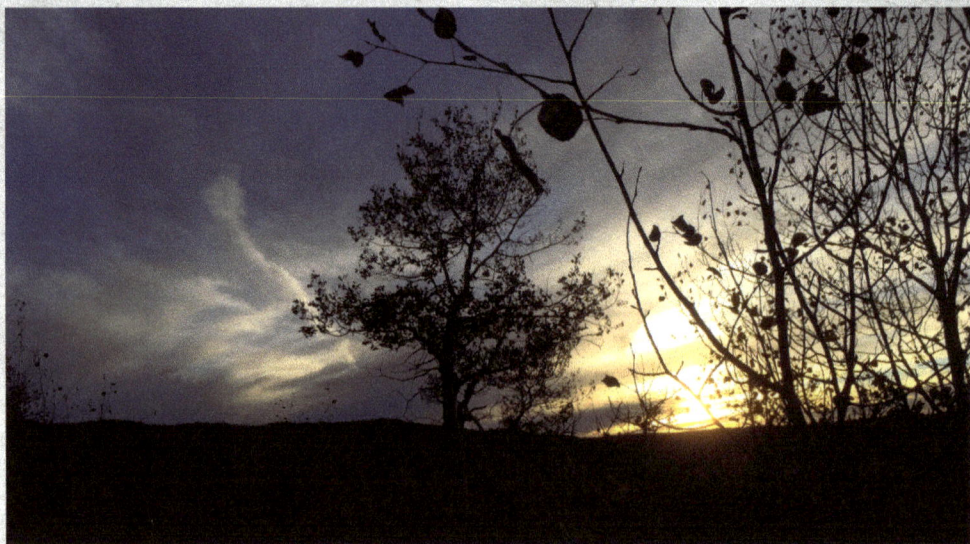

Re-Thinking Thought

"What is the source of all this trouble?...I'm saying that the source is basically in thought."

—DAVID BOHM, *THOUGHT AS A SYSTEM*

NOT ONLY ASSUMPTIONS MUST BE QUESTIONED, but the very tools with which we question. In the same manner as Einstein upended our understanding of time and space, physicist David Bohm brought into question our manner of thinking and, consequently, our every perception.

Bohm is recognized as one of the great scientific innovators of the 20th century. His investigations into the quantum realm moved quantum science from its early mechanical approach into a radically new and successful direction. Bohm's unconventional view focused on an underlying, non-deterministic reality from which quantum activity springs. These progressive theories on quantum science became the basis of his later theses on the nature of reality (*The Implicate Order*) and on the nature of human thought (*Thought as a System*).

Bohm's theory on human thought maintains that it is part of a large, shared system operating upon us. We do not choose to think our thoughts, nor do we evaluate situations based upon information that thought provides. Instead, according to Bohm: "*It* runs *you*. Thought runs you. Thought, however, gives the false information that you are running it, that you are the one who controls thought, whereas actually thought is the one which controls each one of us."

To better understand, let us consider briefly each component of the thought-system in Bohm's theory.

First, Bohm asserts that human thought is essentially a *set of reflexes*. We learn by storing a thought, with any associated emotions and bodily reactions, into memory. Memory registers them in the form of a collective reflex. For example, when we are frightened by a snake as a child, we register the entire experience into memory. Later in life, when a different snake appears, this multi-faceted experience leaps upon us without consent. We react from memory, not act from thought. In fact, Bohm contends that the large majority of what we believe to be new thoughts are repetitions of prior thoughts and emotions. This memory-reflex system assists us in performing daily tasks without the need to relearn and in making regular decisions without the need to reevaluate. However, as these thought patterns repeat over time, they become inflexible. Thoughts vigorously demand repetition, and the force of the thoughts and related emotions are extremely difficult to overcome. Our actions become reactions, even when they clearly do not fit the situation.

We need only look around to find evidence of hardened thought systems. With elderly individuals who have lived a lifetime of repeated patterns, we witness irritation over the slightest interruption to their conditioned world. In old and young alike, we notice emotionally charged behavior seemingly unconnected to current circumstances. This reflex component of thought is also the focus of recent research into substance addiction. A popular catch-phrase in addiction science is "Cells that fire together, wire together." Addiction is produced from a pattern of brain activity that the substance induces. This creates a "fired wire"—an automatic, overwhelming reflex which springs unwanted upon the addict. In a similar manner, Bohm asserts that a repetitive thought produces an unwanted fired wire demanding inflexible behavior.

This inflexibility multiples immeasurably when the memory involves trauma. Even everyday events can unpredictably connect to the trauma, and its multi-faceted horror leaps from hiding. The intensity of emotion cannot be resisted. The falseness of the reality projected onto present circumstances cannot even be glimpsed. The trauma is relived again and again.

While dominant, the reflex nature of human thought is not its only trait. A second attribute, according to Bohm, is that thought *inherently organizes everything*. Its nature is to objectify and, as such, to structure reality into divisions. Our thoughts create categories that may or may not exist in reality. An example is thought itself. Thought tells us that it is separate from our emotions and our body while, in operation if not in fact, these three are intimately entwined. Another example is the distinct division it makes between pleasure and pain when these states are typically experienced as fluctuating mixtures. More dangerously, thought divides humanity into nations, religions, racial groups, political parties, social classes and endless other categories, thus creating conflict and discord.

Next, and importantly, the thought system *creates perceptions*. Thoughts look for and find facts reinforcing their imposed view of reality. One example is the "halo effect" on our perceptions when we fall in love. Not only one's lover, but everyone and everything is suddenly bathed in beautiful light. People are seen as more kind and generous than before. Conversely, depressive thoughts ruminate on depressive happenings that reinforce them. Our thoughts become our perceptions. Reality is rendered like a mirror reflecting our ideas of reality.

Finally, the thought system *struggles against itself*, against all the unpleasant consequences of its inherent nature. Thought does not like the dysfunction caused by its rigid reflexes; it does not like the conflicts that its forced divisions create; and it does not like that its subjective perception of reality—its *reality*—is not shared by all. In response, the thought system employs the same system functions that created the problems to correct them. To address dysfunction, conflict and disharmony, we introduce rigidity, division and the rightness of subjective perception. Bohm describes this as a "systemic fault" in the entire thought system, inevitably leading to a state of "sustained incoherence."

What can we do? Bohm advocated a communication technique known as the Bohm Dialogue. The method attempts to bring awareness to the defective aspects of thought by inserting periods of space and silence into our discussions. We allow a suspension of judgment before reentering the conversation. This space permits conflicting opinions and opposing realities to exist without demanding resolution. Bohm likened this suspended state to the distress experienced by Isaac Newton before his great discoveries. Newton must have suffered significant unease in the confusion of seemingly unsolvable scientific puzzles. Rather than demanding an immediate answer so to be relieved of this troubled state, however, Newton permitted himself to remain in distress without certitude. According to

Bohm, only by accepting incoherence and conflict and by suspending immediate judgment can true answers rise.

Like his quantum particles whose margins are approximations only, whose natures are quasi-autonomous, Bohm encourages us to practice loosening our boundaries. To put less faith in our thought-perceptions. We breathe space around them *while we think them*. We pause and allow our thoughts to be less hardened. We ourselves—the one perceiving—may also become less defined. In this in-between space, within the tension of undefined opposites and undeclared truths, we await discovery.

One remaining attribute of the thought system has not yet been discussed: Thought *generates thought*. Despite its current deficiencies, the system is under constant re-generation. One person's thought becomes another's and vice versa and interplays with a third's in explosive resonances. Like the slightest impress into the thicket left by a single stray deer, others are drawn to it and the impress widens exponentially into a path. The slightest deviation in how a deer travels creates a path. The slightest deviation in how a person thinks creates a movement. There is great hope.

Interactivity

A SIMULTANEOUS WORLD THRIVES within our everyday one.

In addition to his work in quantum physics and human thought, David Bohm introduced the notion of reality-as-interactivity. He showed his students a simple house plant with its classical spatial dimensions of stem, branches, leaves and roots. As such, the plant was presented as existing within defined margins. It was also presented as existing within defined time as it grows and withers over a particular lifespan. However, the physicist was able to offer an alternative reality for his plant. Once a humble seed in soil, the plant breathed in and assimilated all of its elements from outside of the seed. The roots and stem and leaves which developed are not the plant, according to Bohm. The plant is instead a dynamic continuous interplay of "self" and "not-self" and the two are quite indistinguishable. While the plant assimilates ingredients from its environment and assembles itself, it also disassembles and disperses what was plant into not-plant. Furthermore, despite its apparent lifespan, the plant-as-activity is not sequential either. Its interplays are more mutual than progressive and, as mutual, the direction of the plant is incalculable. The plant is dynamized in every possible direction. Its three-dimensional spatial outline only approximates its vigorous reality, its hidden assimilations and disassimilations. Every pore is opened. Becoming and unbecoming. Drawn in and out of. A participation. A relationship.

An utterly irreplaceable ongoing creation.

Bohm described this alternative reality as akin to river waters where vortices form and persist in more or less stable arrangements. In the same manner, the plant represents a stable pattern in the flux of existence, appearing to the human eye to be separated from its environment. Yet even these arrangements of matter and energy are constantly fed by the flux and feed the flux. Bohm asks: what is the boundary of a pattern which is stable yet which unceasingly interchanges itself with its surroundings?

All of reality moves in relationship. Something comes alive, becomes an involvement between the self and the world. Something which cannot be measured. Its margins unfixed.

This sense of interchange and belonging may be experienced in the natural happenings of life. In dance, for example, one allows the music to enter the body and relate with it in a living involvement. The music gifts its audible beat and rhythm while the body gifts its synchronizing physical motions in a mutual harmony. The interaction exists in a place separate from the music or the body. A living place between the two where neither is eliminated. Each is alive in and a part of the other. Lovemaking too allows an opening into this place, where touch and being touched mix in surrendering of self and assimilation of other. We sense a simultaneous loss and finding of oneself. We come alive.

A simple practice for experiencing this reality is merely to pause and notice nature. Wherever we are, we look up and see and listen to any small aspect. Broken sunlight splinters through cloud or leaf, its patches of light and shadow shifting. Squirrels or ants engage in exchanges with earth, or grasses sway within the play of breezes. Stars quiver through winter air. Each in relationship with the other. In relationship, too, with us. We sense its innocence, and our spirit moves within its subtle rhythms. We connect in an exchange that cannot be described with mere names and words. A collaboration ignites.

As with contours of snow in rolls across the winter landscape. Layers of shadow against the stately white. Gusts newly arriving play within and about the moldable shapes. Snow pebbles lift on bands of wind while winds settle through pebbles of snow. Spools of light and dark sparkle everywhere in meagerness. They mass and disperse. They speak to one another in whispers. Asking. Receiving.

Like wine assimilating the flavors of its unique grape, water and barrel, the self becomes a drinking in and drunken from. Of tasting and becoming, of being tasted and unbecoming. A moving mixture of mutualities. The dynamic at the edge. Self spreads and absorbs outside of self. Even life is passed to life, unbecomes but does not die. So deeply a part. So tied together. So poetic. A vibrant exchange of breath and beauty.

O' to sail beyond the seeable margins, the horizon. To break into the wide, the alive. Breathing life into and out of the world. To rupture the chains of objective time and meaning. Naming ourselves beyond ourselves, out in the passages where we meet and share our lives.

Outside ourselves are we born.

"Come my friends," as the poet Tennyson entreated. "Tis not too late to seek a newer world." Let us venture beyond the shores of sun and stars into the vast unknown. To break forth and sail out. To leave the comfort of hearth and known. To sail past where the celestial stars sink into the deep. Past the arc of margins, to the world beyond, knowing not if we will ever return.

Universal Pain

IN FACING OUR MISPERCEPTIONS, we come to recognize our pain.

The first to turn the lens of science upon the inner, unseen workings of human psychology was Sigmund Freud. He theorized at length on possibilities of our psychological structures: the id, ego and super-ego, consciousness and subconsciousness, complexes and drives. Much of Freud's thinking currently suffers disfavor, particularly his belief that psychological healing requires visits into an individual's subconscious past. Yet still esteemed is Freud's initial insight that we are not objective, logical beings. We are instead driven by defensive mechanisms put in place during our formative childhood years. Human behavior is dominated by subconscious compulsions that have little to do with current reality. We perceive a world embedded from the past. Hidden from us, these dominating drives are experienced as important truths and needs, as identity, as survival itself.

According to Freud, a child from the very onset and result of birth suffers great anxiety. We appear to be biologically wired to sense threats of danger, whether real or imagined. Fear of the dark, of monsters under the bed, or of separation from a parent. Anxiety is a signal, experienced as pressing tension, that action is necessary to thwart the danger. However, a powerless child is incapable of thwarting the threat and so, to relieve the anxiety, employs psychological tools that distort or deny reality. Faced with a frightening or unacceptable situation, a child may repress the distressing fact (the fear or shame is relieved by denying that it ever happened), may project it (rather than facing what is unacceptable, it is seen as happening elsewhere or existing in others), may regress (the child falls back to a safer stage of development), may isolate (the child withdraws attention from reality), or may employ splitting (unable to reconcile good and bad, reality becomes harshly polarized). Numerous other defense mechanisms exist.

Important to Freud's theories is that these psychological defenses are employed by all children, not just those experiencing trauma. The strategies are universally applied to protect ourselves against inherent anxieties, which then become embedded in our psyche. While neurosis may develop in some—an exaggeration of the defense mechanism to such a degree that it affects functioning—everyone possesses entrenched defensive techniques we default to throughout life. From our childhood experiences, we are dominated by hidden fears and psychological responses that tend to distort reality and create conflict. Mechanisms which vigorously resist discovery. We hold to our secret distortions in preference to the pain unfiltered reality may bring.

For those in need of help, recent treatments have proven effective, including cognitive behavioral therapy (CBT) and dialectical behavioral therapy (DBT), among others. Freud's theories on childhood fears and defenses bring to light our hidden compulsions and thus a path to treatment and recovery.

For everyone, these theories offer something else as well. Perhaps, a more intimate understanding of pain. Under Freud's thinking, pain is not linearly caused. It exists inherently. Suffering thus cannot be compartmentalized as "out there" and subject to control and avoidance. Fear, dysfunction and conflict arise from the fact of birth. In realizing this, our judgments and manipulations of reality soften. There arises a possibility of being at peace with pain. Instead of fighting it, as seeing it as objectively separate from us, we come to accept it as innate and unavoidable. We are part of the pain and, in reconciling with this truth, there is healing.

A reconciliation with pain. A deepening sense of its origins—the rigid patterns and psychological defenses inseparable from our nature. As we begin to recognize the past revolving into the present, all judgment falls away. There is forgiveness for others or, rather, no need to forgive. Forgiveness too for our own failings, or no need to forgive ourselves. A breathy allowing of the truth of pain. Peace in pain, in existence impossible without it.

Mindfulness

THE FIRST AND EVER-RECURRING CHALLENGE is our suffering. It comes in a myriad of forms: loss, anger, anxiety, loneliness, physical ailments and many more. It is here, in suffering, where the self is finally encountered and experienced.

One guide offering aid is mindfulness. Yet what is mindfulness? The term is used in several ways, often to sell products and services having little to do with its nature. To Jon Kabat-Zinn, a prominent psychologist who developed the popular Mindfulness Based Stress Reduction program, this question must begin with what it is not. Mindfulness is not an absence of thought, not a meditative calmness and not an in-the-moment bliss.

The current popularity of mindfulness may be based on any number of misconceptions drawing people to it. Once exposed to the practice, though, it takes hold as something marvelously different. This is mindfulness: the opening of a window to our own dominating thoughts and emotions, thus to our own suffering. It is a light inside the dark mental cave from which hidden content springs upon us. Moods and distressing thoughts, reflexive emotions and physical pain. With practice, mindfulness teaches us to not identify with what appears to be our own emotions and thoughts. Instead of living from within them, we practice looking at them as separate from us. We give them space to be and to move. We watch as our disappointment, anger, blame or—dare we, our fears—rise and travel through us. Or even more difficult, we give space and attention to our own violence. We look at the pain we so desperately long to bury. Where does it exist physically? Is the belly hardening? Are other muscles tightening? What name would you give to this pain? Does it change in intensity? Does it move? Permit it freedom. Watch it. Allow it to be, with space. Or, better yet, with compassion.

Yes, that would be the ultimate description of mindfulness: to finally forgive our pain. To accept it with softness.

This practice of mindfulness opens the possibility of a wider approach. Perhaps, we begin to observe an entire thought-mood system that is itself suffering. An objective system that separates us from life but is itself separate from us. A self-reflective world of our own mental ideas. The practice is the same, yet wider. We watch and allow, with space, our hardening of reality. Our judgments, evaluations and labeling. All the truths we tell ourselves. We notice the tightness in the belly, the franticness of mental rules and rightness. We give it space, allow a breathiness around it. A softening, not of the hardness, but toward it. Toward all of it—the larger mental network defining and pressurizing our world.

Something beautiful thrives outside our thought-mood system. Something genuine. In the first glimmerings of forgiveness, we touch the first glimmerings of *reverence*.

Death

Imagine, if you will, receiving news of your approaching death. What is your reaction? It may seem impossible to imagine such a traumatic experience and to predict your response. As you think about it, though, you may say things to yourself about what you "think" will occur. I think I will love and worry about my family. I think (or hope) that I will not have regrets. I think I will miss walks in the woods and dogs and morning coffee. There are endless variations of reactions I imagine, but these are not the reactions likely to occur.

Here is a hint to what may actually occur: there will be deep grieving. Even if you have lived what you believe to be a satisfying life. Even if you have faith in God who has guided you through tough times, or you have loved and been loved fully. The blessings *of faith or love surely soften the end, yet you are still likely to suffer painful grieving, not for the reason of your death or your life, but for the reason of thought itself, our paradigm lens. You have lived your entire life seeking and holding to certainties. Facts and truths and plans to be pursued. A better description might be comfort, the comfort of something tangible you can hold to. The comfort of understanding things so they are predictable and reassuring. But that predictability has just left the room. All that is left in this room is you and your thoughts, and your thoughts are demanding the comfort of understanding. But what understanding is possible when all is ending?*

With future and progression suddenly taken, you are unsure of who you are, or have been. Your thoughts will rewind through the past to try to name you and your life. They will demand it. What is, or has been, the meaning of all of this? Who am "I", here departing this world unaccompanied? What remains? Ideas whirl through your head as to who you think you are and what your life has meant. Yet nothing hides from death, and the abrupt, unfair end of everything brings the shallow to light. Not your life as shallow, but the thoughts that limit it, that thereby trivialize it. You realize the triviality and may mistake it for your life. Is that all I am, you ask. Just things I've accomplished? Roles I've played? Definitions of me? Has it meant anything? You will realize in the depths of your soul that no comfort of meaning exists. Despite all denials, despite your thoughts' pleading voice that your life matters, the lack of understanding descends, and the grieving begins.

Some people believe conclusions such as these should be hidden from the dying because they foster depression. Yet have these same people also insisted that you are not dying, and for the same reason? Does insisting you are not dying relieve depression or worsen it? Does denying the lack of meaning assist the dying or plunge them deeper into falseness and triviality? The Great Uncertainty is descending. All your certitudes are being taken. Will you grasp at a last desperate thought-certainty as your final futile act? There is no certainty! No comfort of knowing! Does it not feel better to face this reality, like death, and to fully taste its living flavor? Grieve not the loss of "you" but grieve instead the loss of certainty, of understanding. Grieve them and see their fragile underpinnings. With the end of everything known fast approaching, the farce of life-as-thought is finally challenged. The idea of the future has been stolen, which suddenly renders all ideas vulnerable.

In grieving the loss of ideas, though, the blessings of the loss of ideas begin to flow. The blessings of utter uncertainty. Unpredictability need not be scary; it is real, alive, urgently in front of you and inviting you to live it. There is no tomorrow to shape. There is no world to right. Without the clutter of a future to plan, you are free to touch and ride the untamed adventure you are entering. Not untamed as meaningless; not uncertainty as random chance. And not waiting on the other side of the grave either, but here, now. Real.

Who you are and what your life means cannot be found like some rigid truth or law. It's just more thought-stuff. So inherently unfulfilling. So limiting. So false, cold and trivial when tested at death's gate. So we allow the loss of our ordered ideas and, finally, there is order. We begin to see through the uncaring, objective thought-order around us into the natural, beautiful ordering that is life. Tears may fall in the realization of so much goodness; deep satisfying goodness. Meaning is not a thing that can be named or explained but is our part in the living goodness. We suddenly know who we are without the fragile props of personal justification. Alive, even in death. A bridge that ties us together, that ties all together. In this moment, we become part of a dynamic ordering and goodness. A living place we enter, contributing to a widening, vibrant eternity. Death cannot touch us.

Must we wait for death's call to come alive?

Spiritual Genius

JESUS DESCRIBED THE COMING of the kingdom of heaven as a journey. In the parable of the prodigal son, a father has two sons, the elder being dutiful, the younger reckless. The rebellious younger son demands his inheritance and uses it to travel extravagantly in distant lands. His money soon spent, he falls into degradation and despair. Utterly lost, the son scratches at the bottom of this foreign land for the barest of sustenance. Gone is his prior world of certainty and identity. Jesus does not tell us how long the prodigal son wanders in misery, but he tells us of a strange occurrence there. Unexpectedly, in the midst of his pain, the prodigal son awakens to a mysterious gift. It bids him to return home but not to regain his former status. He returns, but transformed somehow, longing to be a poor servant. His father embraces the boy deeply in his arms and calls for a feast, for the long-broken home is finally reunited. Surprisingly, though, the parable does not end here. To prevent any misinterpretation of the kingdom of heaven, the parable continues. Everyone in the entire estate is invited to the feast, but the elder son refuses to attend, claiming that his younger brother is unworthy of such celebration. With incredible irony, Jesus explains how the most deserving, the son who dutifully worked the fields in his brother's absence, is the one absent from the kingdom of heaven. The obedient son is wholeheartedly invited, but he excludes himself because of his mental trappings.

This son remains in a world of favor or rejection. He has not entered the lost lands and is thus incapable of receiving its gifts.

Is it possible this parable arose from a journey Jesus himself endured? After identified as the messiah by John the Baptist, Jesus withdraws to pray in the desert. We are told how, in the temptations suffered there, he is enticed to live as would the expected messiah. Satan tempts him: "If you are the son of God,..." take control, rise up into greatness, overthrow the oppressor. In the medium of the disorienting desert, however, Jesus sheds the traditional understanding of the messiah and is gifted a deeper meaning of himself and his mission. A new type of messiah is revealed of a new type of order. Immediately upon his return from the desert, he announces the coming of the kingdom of heaven. The dominant world of "greatness" and "chosen" has faded, and a very different world has opened. A kingdom of forgiveness where the "little ones" and the "least" dwell. Where the child and child-like enter, the blameless of spirit regardless of all failings of behavior. Where failings are instead visible, universal and humbling. The advent of a reality celebrating the tiniest mustard seed and insignificant pinch of yeast as its vital spark.

Before Christianity, this pattern was mirrored for centuries in the rites of the Eleusinian Mysteries. The rites reenacted the journey of Demeter, who descends into the dark underworld, travels its perilous paths in search for her abducted daughter, and ultimately reunites with her daughter and is resurrected back to earth. While details of the secret rites remain veiled in mystery, it is believed that initiates symbolically died, wandered a nocturnal underworld and were reborn at dawn. The actions of the initiates, like those of Demeter, follow the eternal pattern of life: the summer field which descends into long winter so that its seeds may ignite from their shells and rise into spring.

In the sixth century BCE, Siddhartha Gautama sought to break the shell of human suffering. He turned from wealth and ease to become a holy wanderer across India's Ganges Plain in search of the answer to humanity's painful condition. Legend holds that, shortly before his enlightenment, Gautama renounced the prevailing spiritual traditions and embraced a "middle path" between extremes. Content with neither the rigors of asceticism nor the serenity of yoga states, Gautama drifted aimlessly for the elusive way to break the pattern of suffering in this life. Ultimately, he sat himself beneath the fabled Bodhi Tree vowing to gain an answer or to die there. On the forty-ninth day of meditation under the tree, Gautama is said to have touched his hand to the earth as a lightning bolt of awakening shook through him, experiencing his true nature within the true nature of the universe. Gautama, who became known by his followers as Buddha, or Awakened One, began to teach a way to splinter our hardened structure of craving and passions. Through practices of meditation, attention and lifestyle, we loosen our conditioned state so to rise into the joy of our true nature. We live free of our rigid shell. Free of suffering! Such is the path of Buddha, the Awakened One.

The ancient Chinese philosopher Lao Tzu was journeying past the last threshold of society—the far western gate of China—when stopped by a sentry at the wall. Before your death to this world, the sentry pleaded, write down your wisdom so that those you leave behind may yet prosper. The noble sage consented, discoursing through 81 chapters of the *Tao Te Ching* on the nature of the Way, or Tao. The Way is like water, he wrote, ever-flowing to the lowest place "that others reject" and, from this place, nourishing life. Like water, it "cares for all things and does not compete with them." The Tao, similar to an archer's bow, brings low what is high and raises high what is low. The Tao does not judge, for by defining the beautiful, you create the ugly. Those who know the Tao cannot say what it is; those who say what it is cannot know. The Tao is close to the land and deep in the heart, but to try to name it or to hold it is to lose it. The Tao cannot be sought, for it will elude your capture. Only the humble and simple understand: you cannot take the Tao to yourself; you can only give yourself to the Tao. Given over, you enter a land of goodness free of personal merit, of innocence outside of individual virtue, of essence beyond any imagining.

The revered Prophets of ancient Hebrew tradition were scorned for their difficult message of humbling repentance as the path of rescue from oppression. Such too was the example of the world-rejuvenating Krishna of the great Hindu tradition, who taught of "selfless service" as the way to freedom from the chains of the material. And likewise humanity's last Holy Prophet, Muhammed, who carried to the world a single over-whelming message: absolute self-surrender.

Spiritual genius guides not only history but progeny. It calls to us. It is time.

Loss. Disorientation. Surrender. Essence.

The Lost King

THE THEME OF THE LOST KING runs throughout human history. Odysseus endlessly thwarted in his return from the Trojan War as his kingdom suffers under charlatan rule. King Richard the Lionheart astray in far Crusades while his homeland falls into tyranny, eased only by Robin Hood and his band of misfit heroes. The Fisher King, whose mind is lost due to deathly wounds as his kingdom turns to waste. More recently, Aragorn (of *The Lord of the Rings*) and the Lion King are banished while their kingdoms darken in anarchy. In each tale, the reign descends into ruin for lack of its rightful king, who after endless forgotten years returns and the kingdom is reborn.

The Lost King echoes in our everyday world as well. Jungian psychologists utilize the theme as exemplifying the psychological journey of "individuation." Individuation is a term coined by famed psychologist Carl Jung to describe the process of separation, transition and reintegration that he believed all personal transformation entails. The first step on this journey—separation—involves a recognition of the falseness of current reality. Like Queen Penelope who aches for the return of Odysseus, one realizes that present times are under a reign of misrule. To Jung, the modern person suffers in a similar false reality, a mechanical world rising from humanity's overemphasis on the rational half of its psyche.

Jungian psychologist Murray Stein, in his book *In Midlife: A Jungian Perspective*, equates our modern mechanical reality with ancient Troy at the time of its fall. Sensing the end of their world, the beautiful Andromache pleads with her husband, Prince Hektor, to refuse Achilles' challenge to a battle of death. She seems to understand the threat this duel poses to all of Troy. Yet Hektor knows himself only as a warrior-hero and is compelled to conform to his structured role. In Homer's epic poem *The Iliad*, Hektor explains to his wife:

I would feel deep shame…
if like a coward I were to shrink aside from the fighting;
and the spirit will not let me, since I have learned to be valiant
and to fight always among the foremost ranks of the Trojans,
winning for my own self great glory, and for my father.

(Homer, Iliad 6.442-446)

To himself, Hektor *is* his stereotyped image and its dominance blinds him to the consequences of his decision, which Andromache so painfully sees. For more than Hektor's death lies ahead. When Hektor is slain in the contest, his nation and its self-identifications die with him. A funeral pyre is prepared for Troy's last great prince, foretelling the coming destruction of Troy entire. This is the beginning of the journey. A crumbling of a known world opening to the entry of another. The coming reintegrated world is still a distant whisper, though, and the current reality is harsh separation. A painful end to known identities. The good king and his reign are gone, lost. We enter into transition lands, a world referred to in Jungian circles as liminality. The liminal is the thresholds, the in-betweens, the borderlands. The neither here nor there. Disorientation abounds, but there is no returning to the old. A funeral pyre has honored the death of the old, and we must grieve and let go. There is only the journey ahead.

The process of individuation enters its transition stage. We are off the safe King's Highway into the wooded and unknowable hinterlands. Stein again uses the myth of the Lost King to illustrate this phase of individuation. He refers to King Odysseus' journeys and the repeated attempts to return to his homeland. Storms, seductive plants and goddesses, hypnotizing songs and arbitrary fates all work to block his forward course. At the same time, Odysseus is aided by an array of guides, gifts and wisdom from the realm of the gods. For Stein and his Jungian perspective, these gifts are part of the lost lands and can be found nowhere else. Foremost among these gifts is the messenger god Hermes, who crosses the borderlands separating humanity from the gods to aid the wandering Odysseus. Hermes provides a serum to counter the charms of the enchantress Circe and leads Odysseus through the unnavigable underworld to learn the secrets of wise Tiresias.

Like Odysseus, we too are lost without bearings as we enter the transitional phase of individuation seeking a genuine homeland. Our former certainties have left us. Prior convictions are suddenly viewed as wrongful; a type of misrule has usurped the rightful king. There is suffering in this loss, but something is freed as well. The soul is no longer constrained in hierarchies, customs or expectations. The pursuit of what others believe to be desirable and respectable is now seen as trivial. A deepness calls, but from where and to what remains unclear. In such a state, according to Jungian thought, we can despair and cling to former certainties, despite their seeming falseness, or we can allow ourselves to be guided through these lands. We are to look for the guide of the lost, the leader of souls through Hades, the maker and breaker of boundaries, the herald between gods and humanity, that creative inventor and misfit thief, the incomparable, mythological Hermes.

To Jung and the psychological movement he inspired, the Greek god Hermes represents the ultimate nature of the transitional lost lands. Like the wand always found in his hand—his caduceus—Hermes is a dynamic synthesis of opposites. The caduceus prominently displays two mirrored snakes writhing up its pole, until a keen observer realizes that the snakes are not mirrored images but are instead opposites, male and female, completing each other. The helix they form looks startlingly similar to the doubled DNA helix of opposing strands. As a bond between contradictions, Hermes and his wand become a symbol of origins, of new beginnings. Jung's vision of transcendent space captures this same dynamic. Intense conflict and painful paradox dominate, but if one can hold to the tension without choosing one side over the other, a "third space" is created.

In this third space, contradictions which previously defined our reality become confused. The opposites no longer oppose; instead they join. They exist together in some odd bond which cannot be comprehended but can be experienced. Archetypes rise, symbols from a hidden mystery world. The everyday is widened, in a way, to include indefinable offerings from another reality. Scarabs, dragons and pyramids; tricksters, outcasts and heroes. These are psychic experiences which cannot nor should not be explained. Highly unlikely but meaningful coincidences, or synchronicities, arrive unexpectedly. Dreams seem larger and significant, despite their confusing messages. These occurrences are not offered for comprehension, however. They do not represent a clear path toward transformation. As mysteries from the subconscious, they offer no rational understanding and, consequently, forge no road that can be followed. They are merely energy. A pulse and flow which may be life-giving and at times guiding, although never fully understood.

What then can be understood in this land? Does it offer any substance for comfort after the loss? No, none, according to Jung, for the third space is not a replacement realm, not a new world. Not yet. It is a lost world where nothing can or should be held to, for to choose one of two opposing contradictions is to remain in the prior objective world. We are to disavow the wrongful kings—the "truths" everywhere demanding recognition of their rightness. We know not if the rightful king will ever appear. He may be long dead on some distant battlefield. Nothing is certain, yet uncertainty and upheaval are an acceptable choice over certainty and hollowness. We accept that we cannot go back, although the prevailing experience is one of suffering, for clarity has been stolen and a reign of misrule ravages the land.

Over time, a sense of receptivity gradually replaces a need for understanding. The third space creates a loosening of objective reality, but also contains a seed of something new. This too is represented in Hermes' caduceus as a set of wings sits atop the two helixed snakes, like a child perched to fly from the joining of its polar parents.

Does the Lost King ever return? Is a profound transformation ever realized? Both Jung and myth tell us yes, that the rightful king eventually steps upon his long-departed shore. He travels the kingdom in disguise to learn of its loyalties and treacheries. The king is then revealed and the kingdom wholly reborn. As such—and this is important to note—the reborn kingdom is not the painful third space without truth, nor any prior space of certain truth, but is a land of new and yet unknowable truth. A wondrous new beginning.

Grieving into Belonging

We are launched upon the waters. Tossed to every side as our world unhinges from its moorings. Crises snatch away our dreams and meaning. We are left with an emptiness groaning as for breath, and we cry out for peace. Peace, I pray!

Yet what is peace? Is it the answer we envision in our prayers? An easing of the turmoil, where we can relax in an orderly calm that surrounds and showers us like a soothing summer rain? This admittedly sounds nice. The problem lies in its reliance on a world that does not exist. As we have explored, pain and conflict are inherent to birth. Nonlinear turns are natural to nearly every system. If we equate peace with orderly calm, we will experience much unrest.

Even if we may not realize it, each of us has a choice. In the midst of heartbreak and turmoil, we can continue to yearn for peace in a peaceful world, or we can begin to realize peace in a riotous world.

If this were true, though, would not everyone make a decision for lasting peace? Sadly no, for lasting peace is known by other names as well. Names such as disorder, or perhaps darkness, even death. As though lost on the blackest of nights in the loneliest of places, the tendency is to fight the blackness, to demand a light to guide us home. This search for light is not peace, though; it is fright. As we frantically pitch through the darkness pleading for light, another possibility is gathering in the fragments of our *desperation: there is no light! There exists no certainty in all of the world. There is only black of night, only confusion and lostness. The idea of future and direction has been radically severed. There is here. There is now. There is a choice to enter the helplessness of the night.*

Disconnection is considered the cause of the world's problems, but false, fragile connections appear to wreak the greater havoc. Everything and everyone is connected to an idea as to what it represents. A friend, for example, is connected to a set of expectations as to how the friend should act. When they violate this connection to the idea, the friend must be scolded and the identity mended. If the connection cannot be restored, the friend is given a new identity, perhaps even enemy. Our mind demands a connection to an identification that is separate from who or what the other really is.

So many things may seem broken or breaking but, possibly, it is these representations that are breaking down. Others no longer serve the purpose or represent the idea we have placed on them. As our world becomes increasingly chaotic, the assurance of what the other represents begins to crumble. We are losing the certainty of our definitions, and the pain of these disconnections is real. Our paradigm has relied on objective references for the world to make sense. We have depended on linear, sequential time to understand and shape our world. Yet the swirling turmoil is weakening these comforts of certainty. No identification is holding true. No expectation is holding firm. Nothing is holding still at all. We cannot evaluate. We cannot understand. Only complete uncertainty reigns.

Are we left with nothing then? Yes, nothing. From the viewpoint of our logical paradigm, all landmarks have vanished. Our world has ended. Plans and hopes have been ripped away. Everything appears disjointed from any continuity. Chaos is stealing our world from us. In this realization there is great sadness. The sadness is genuine and must not be dismissed as trite. How could one lose a sense of understanding and not experience great grief? We must say goodbye, and it is natural for goodbyes to be hard. The old order is passing away, and the time has come for tears.

With this grieving, though, slowly and subtly, a soft realization dawns. The departing world and its complete focus on identifications created an artificial world. They enclosed our reality in a sequestered order, an enforced order. Boxed in, as though in a square windowless room, anxious from the deafening clutter. Our days were overfilled with racing and distress, anxiety and insincerity, conflict and confusion. Even convictions which previously held so much meaning reveal themselves as false. Forgeries, for they offer nothing but more of the same. They have been co-opted into service of a hard-structured world and only further its emptiness. Every thought and emotion seems practiced, as though we've been there before and it doesn't work. None of it. Absolutely none of our objective perceptions work, or make sense, or matter.

It is at this point, as these indefinable yet undeniable realizations float upward through our grief, that the clarity of day begins to turn to the mystery of night. We honor disconnection; that is, allow another to exist without a rigid identity chained to them. We permit a disconnection with the definition and we choose to honor the other over the identity. Like the beauty of a soft, deepening night, the realization that another may exist separate from an assigned representation is comforting. The moment where we allow the other to live and be alive in and of itself without reference to anything else becomes a moment of aliveness. The other is granted the freedom to be disconnected from our idea of them. They are no more than who and what they are. Everything, _everything_—even if briefly—comes alive in a disjointed way. Each exists and serves a purpose in the very livingness of themselves, in the self-light they radiate.

Can we continue to demand clarity of this world? Do we rely on expectations and identifications? Will we control with answers and dictates? Or might we finally trust the night? Are we able to let go of our mind's need for understanding so to permit each element of the world its own self-meaning, its own self-light? Disjointed from their assigned purpose, are they not just what they are? Can we allow even ourselves to be disjointed from purpose? As though astray in a magical forest, we permit forms and events to appear and disappear without understanding. We assign them no meaning. No required role to play. We breathe. The gloom of goodbyes and loss of clarity loosens, perhaps just a bit, permitting an unexpected sense of freedom to enter. As the despair clears, there emerges a surprising relief. Our fierce rigidness and its urge to push and pull ease. The mental world is breaking down and there is no control of it. There is no solution. Yet there need be none, for the order of control and solution has lost its importance. The unknowable surrounds and showers us like a soothing summer rain.

We let the clear, objective world go and ride into the great uncertainty. We awaken in alertness to the moving present and its dynamic ordering, which feels good, as though a deep goodness dwells within. We touch an open land beyond the narrow road where we have toiled too long. An invisible boundary is passed into a new order, widened, natural as the order of trees. The beauty and meaning for each arise in itself with no reason beyond it. Like the flocks of birds forming and unforming, the watery streams breaking and scattering and gathering anew, the winds swirling beneath fiery autumn leaves, we walk the path of a nonlinear world that turns and swirls with us. Perhaps we feel something, a pulse or a resonating, in the wide sway. We breathe it; we breathe with it. Something beautiful is touched in the vibrant, unknowable present. Something inherently innocent in the people, things, places and events surrounding us. Something we honor above all else. And once touched, nothing can be the same again. Our worth is tied to nothing beyond us. We are disjointed from the clarity of knowledge, alive and moving as part of some teeming goodness. A great innocence, undefiled by the limiting designations of our mind.

A world opens in which we participate. What greater meaning could there be than this? To enter into a living, immediate world of intimate involvement. The peace of belonging to ungovernable life. The deep beauty of unknowable night!

This moment of realization may pass, but we have touched it, and we will never accept the world as before. We may get pulled back into the old order for a time, but we will never again stand with two feet set in that land. We have tasted a new world, and its sweetness ceaselessly beckons us home.

a time of uncertain transition,
of holding to no answer,
of searching,
and of surprising inspirations

Be not afeard; the isle is full of noises,
Sounds, and sweet airs, that give delight and hurt not.
Sometimes a thousand twangling instruments
Will hum about mine ears; and sometime voices,
That, if I then had waked after long sleep,
Will make me sleep again: and then, in dreaming,
The clouds methought would open, and show riches
Ready to drop upon me; that, when I waked,
I cried to dream again.

Awake, dear heart, awake.
Thou hast slept well. Awake.

—WILLIAM SHAKESPEARE, *THE TEMPEST*

The Transition

Confusion, Challenges and Discoveries

Swirling Evolution

CHARLES DARWIN PUBLISHED *On the Origin of Species* in 1859 to much fanfare. His theory of biological evolution through a process of natural selection was widely and quickly acknowledged as significant by the scientific community. Much like the later theory of special relativity posited by Einstein, its popularity was the result of a simplicity of ideas answering a wide scope of questions.

The simple idea was this: The large variety of traits across a population naturally results in selection—that is, those traits better suited to the environment succeed and survive over others. Through reproduction, a large variety of the successful trait proliferates, a small number of which again succeeds and survives over the others. This pattern is repeated through countless generations resulting in billowing new traits and new species successfully adapting to their unique environments. In short, variation results in selection which, through the constant repetition of variation and selection, results in evolution—the creation of species.

A classic example of natural selection is the evolution of bacteria into strands resistant to antibiotic treatments. Bacteria populations contain a huge number of members with a broad variety of traits. When antibiotics were first introduced to kill off bacteria, a small number of bacteria cells possessing traits resistant to the treatment survived. The successful variation (resistant cells)—previously a tiny minority—then reproduced and supplanted the original population. In these and subsequent generations, cells possessing wider variations of the resistant traits were produced, with a minute number possessing even greater resistance to antibiotics. When this next population was exposed to more potent antibiotics, a small minority of the most-resistant cells again survived, repopulated and produced ever-wider variations of the most resistant traits. This process of variation, survival and reproduction, repeated in response to ever-stronger antibiotic treatments over thousands or millions of bacterial generations, created populations of super bacteria—cells completely resistant to antibiotics.

As Darwin noted when first expounding his theory of natural selection, however, evolution is not one-directional as in the bacteria example. He used the image of the Tree of Life to describe his evolutionary theory. Multiple successful traits each spring into a cluster of successful branches, which produce their own sub-branches, and those sub-branches likewise birth sub-sub branches. Amazingly unique qualities billow outward like a tree, multiplying into vastly different functions, species and genera, all related in a commonness of ancestry.

Breakthroughs in science following Darwin provided underlying support for his theory. Studies in genetics found that genes mutate across generations, creating a large variety of the parents' traits. Paleontologists surveying fossils and bones pieced together the unique progression of certain traits into new species. Darwin's theory has itself evolved into one of the cornerstones of science, nearly universally accepted within scientific circles. (And while still disputed in religious circles, it should be noted that natural selection does not necessarily negate a preeminent role for God, only a God who would deny a role for creation.)

Recently, though, evolutionary theorists began to grapple with other questions. They observed that certain of the successful traits created were not additive; that is, the new attribute could not be explained as a variation in shape, size, number or arrangement from the features forming it. The trait possessed completely novel properties seemingly unrelated to the biological material producing it. An example can again be found in bacteria. Scientists observed that a single-celled bacterium possesses what is termed life but that the macromolecules which join to form it do not. The properties of life are foreign to every component interacting to create the bacterium. Yet there it is, suddenly and amazingly alive.

Nature's most precious traits—the hark of sound to the ear or sparkle of light to the eye—are irreducible from the components that comprise them. The function of a pumping heart, as another example, cannot be explained from any element producing it. No heart cell or tissue contains even a hint of its ultimate role. Only the complete heart, with all its miraculously cooperative components, makes a beating heart. Scientists theorize that novel functions and properties rise at critical evolutionary moments, a process referred to as emergence. Interacting components unexpectedly cooperate and spring into a collective operation foreign to its individual parts. Nature leaps into new creations.

While the novel traits sprouting from emergence are impossible to predict, science has identified the conditions that
give rise to these events. Emergent creation requires a great
interconnectivity among large numbers of participants. The
many parts move and interchange with each other without
the restraint of imposed structure. If structured, the relationships would necessarily be linear and, consequently, limited in
scope. Each part would remain in its regulated place relative to
other parts. In the realm of potential emergence, though, all
churns in a decentralized storm, folding and swirling, massing
and dispersing. As distant regions fold inward and out, any
part can interact with any other part, resulting in intense
interconnectivity.

Interconnectivity is not alone sufficient for emergence,
however. Something new is introduced, but that something
is not regulation. No authority leads the incoherence into

coherence. Emergence is not mechanical, not the product of an additive process. It is synergistic, a whole greater than its individual components. Into the storm to spark this synergy arrives *attraction*. A little-known but amazing trait in nature is the tendency of individuals to be attracted to other behavior. Like ants in a colony who are drawn to the trails left by their fellow ants, each action is amplified as an influence for others to follow. This natural attraction produces feedback patterns as the attraction repeatedly doubles an activity's attraction. Mirrored, multiplying behaviors build into cooperative movements, suddenly springing into a functioning opened system.

To better explain, emergence can be thought of as a pot of water atop a stove. Before heat is introduced, the water exists in a stable, yet simple, state. The state is considered simple because it does not support any higher-level function. As the water is heated, the water molecules begin to each pursue an increasing individuality. Each molecule uses the energy introduced to separate itself from stability and to pursue unique preferences and paths. As the heat increases, this individuality rises into a great turbulence. The molecules collide and clash with each other in chaotic interconnectivity. Surprisingly, however, as energy continues to be introduced to the water, individual molecules start to trace the movements of other molecules. These traces attract further followers to the movements in exponentially growing attractions. Suddenly, when a critical threshold is reached, the chaotic water leaps into well-organized convection currents. The molecules work individually in collective harmony.

Convection currents such as these dynamically order the earth's oceans, atmosphere and mantle. This order does not arrive through structure or authority. Feedback attractions create a spontaneous and living *self-order* from disorder. This newly created order is not sequential, but explosive; not additive, but synergistic. Not answer or solution, but birth.

Human interaction possesses these same feedback attraction patterns. For example, one would expect the world's stock markets to act randomly, reflecting the vast number of participants and their individual preferences. In practice, however, participants tend to follow the behavior of other participants and their own behavior attracts further attraction. Investors thus act in exponential waves based on the behavior of other investors. This same dynamic can also be seen in environments of unregulated crowd movements, where people tend to follow others into exponentially enlarging currents of travel. Another example is internet activity, where attraction to a video will "go viral:" that is, attraction to the video itself will double its attraction. Put into situations void of central regulation, humans exhibit a strong tendency to self-organize through feedback attraction patterns.

As already discussed, this same attraction pattern sparks collective intelligence, as with bird flocks and ant colonies and, as will be discussed later, with honeybees.

In most emergent situations, however, the activity does not simply rise and then fall as with an ant's pheromone trail or an internet video. The influence changes as it moves. The diversity through which the influence travels adds its own uniqueness. An example of this dynamic can be found in the evolution of human knowledge.

In the early stages of human development, commercial trade carried interchange outward, fostering more frequent contact between peoples. Principal among these exchanges was thought itself. Truly, the essence of civilization can be viewed as the widening interchange of thought: one person's thought attracting another's and interplaying with a third's into billowing scales of human intelligence. By way of expanding commerce, innovative human ideas rippled through diverse cultures, religions, customs and peoples. As these thoughts

traveled, the innovation innovated. Attraction by others mul-
tiplied the thoughts, but with adjustment, with newness. Like
an exponential game of telephone, the message transforms,
then back it comes through the system, vastly different, influencing even the original influence. Every attraction produces
exponential attraction but reinvigorates and reinvents itself,
returning new as its beginnings. Springing from these vibrant,
diverse connections, startling developments arose in science,
engineering, medicine and just about everything else the mind
could concoct. No longer could thought or action be conceived
as purely individual. It is attractive, shared and explosive.

Swirling creation rises around us. Outside logic or answers,
it brings deregulated movements and amplifying attractions.
A resonance can be sensed within the exchanges, an echoing.
Arrays of ripples reverberating, synchronizing in some magnificent manner. Building to a threshold. Wondrous as the sudden
appearance it produces.

A gift beyond imagining erupts into being.

Wonder

All slows when crossing the threshold…

A first-light blizzard blinds the day's entry. Snow crystals scatter in seemingly every direction at once, with chance outcasts landing at my feet and accumulating one atop other into thousands, then millions, in masses of ladling white. Morning does not rise. Rather, with desperate slowness, it merges into the veiled landscape like a mist wetting all morsels of earth.

I begin with precarious steps forward. Plumes of spinning snow encircle me, halting the visible, the path ahead. Each swarming speck of white twirls upon cups of air in frantic, patternless plays. They dance as to mercurial music fractured and broken. Nothing stands. A shattering of matter not outward or inward, not explosion or implosion. Freed of any forward or reversing momentum. Adplosion—a mad admixture of collapsing upheaval. As I inch forward, my steps rise and fall as though passing through hills of a sort. Contours under my feet turn and flow as would stately dancing gowns. The motion of my uncertain steps seems to be drawing me into the movement. I am walking as upon rippling arrays, teeming pools lit in silver-black bands. My hands open as if to touch swaying meadow grasses, orange-tinged, falling to left then right. My head dizzies in winds which break and fork as though intricate tree branches igniting skyward.

The plans of the day sweep aside in the winds. Only uncertainties come to life. There is no next, then that. All is the living turning variables that arrive and touch at play. Genuine. No fossils vainly stamping upon these seas the names they claim to see, deeming it knowledge. No pressure of chained events. Suddenly separated from the seizing, from the dead of touch, the mechanical. Unraveling the rigid texture of the old world. Such cold, polished shells did that world hold. So filled with fixities. So unlivable. Each of us tied from the neck like a human gear-pin. So scattered when opened to the scattered living storms.

Patterns like clouds form and un-form above the sightless hills. Blurred of vision but awakening of step and motion. I touch each momentary contour as it rolls under or over me every which way. Swirling sweetness surrounds, pervades…receives. Moving, somehow, with the moving world. Lost within a spreading broken stream who knows not a current but instead a thousand, parting into a thousand more glistenings parting anew. No longer thwarted, I seem to be shared in the currents. Oddly and lovely…how I am still my own work and shape but, too, am worked and shaped. I am ending. Such sorrow yet…without sorrow, for I am ending in an irrelevant way. Remembrances of failures fill me, yet so trivial in the light of this new swaying, generous land. As if to lie down in meadows whose seeds, beyond count, teeming, gather me up into the mutable stars. In wonder I lay—we lay—on winds uncontrolled and boundless, fathomless. Ends without endings, for time turns and melds. Irrelevance of ends, uncluttered of structure, of margins which vainly measure beginning and end.

Is it possible? Through tears of heartache, when chaos breaks upon our shore like a terrible wave of sorrow, that the gift of wonder approaches within its spray? So beautiful, to be entered and made a part. Variables turning, branching, swaying us within. Breathing. Adjusting. Then, like a sudden surging tide, wonder washes over us. A pool of misery and miracle, binding us. Do not think. Do not try to understand. For another realm has entered *beyond the structures of time's demand, and there is only belong-ing. Only tears of beauty born.*

Somehow through the spinning winds, a note of birdsong pierces. Stay with me it sings. Stay. Stay…

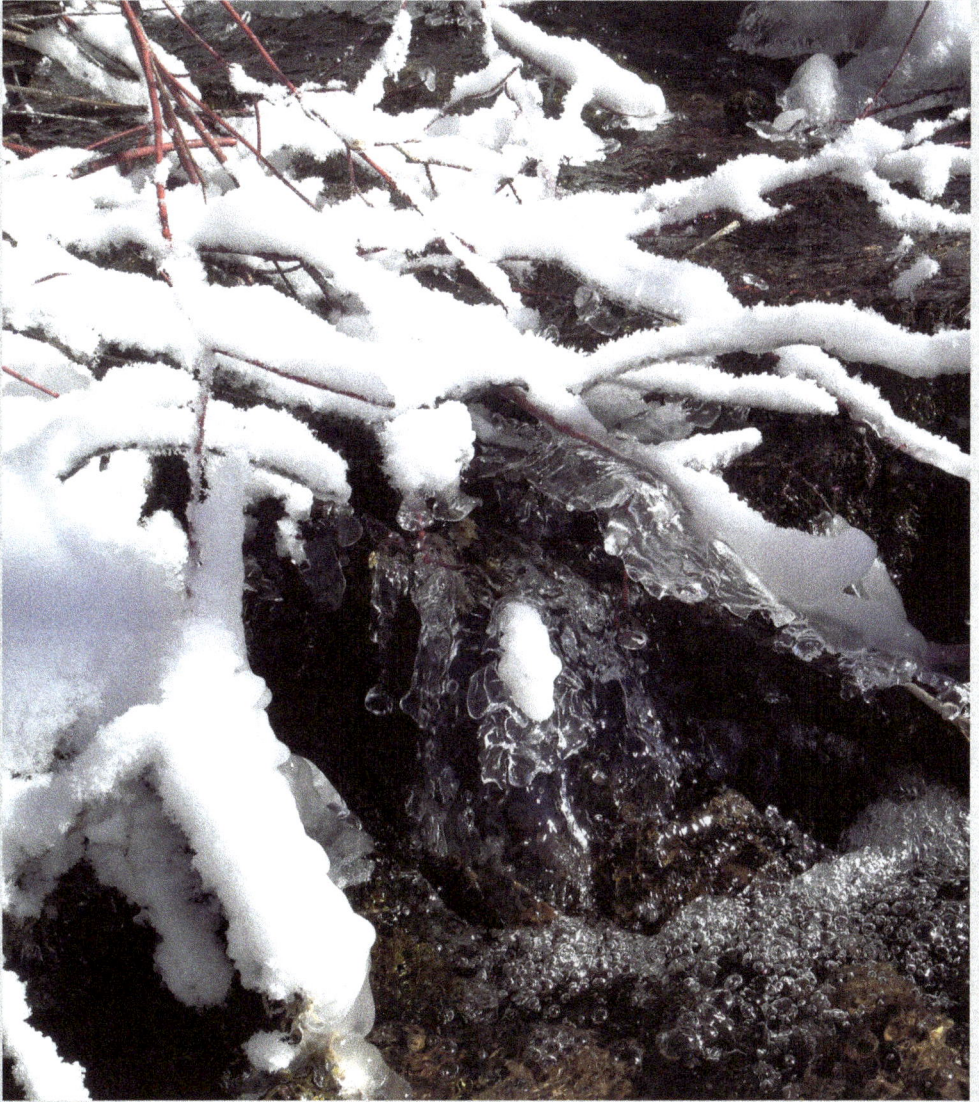

Natural Systems and Human Systems

Say to those whose hearts are frightened:
Be strong, fear not!
Behold, your God is here...
he comes to save you.

Isaiah 35:4

NATURAL SYSTEMS ARE SIMPLE. They involve feedback patterns, each component dynamically taking from and nurturing the whole. The food cycle, the water cycle, the global ocean/wind cycles and countless others re-feeding and re-energizing themselves. Feedback defines nature.

Also, nature's processes are not separate from one another. Each is replenished as part of a larger sustaining network. An organism relies on its ecosystem, which relies on its biome, which relies on its global systems. No cycle operates alone. Each is independent while interdependent.

Another quality of nature worth noting involves the single participant in its workings. From an individual's perspective, nature is ephemeral, each of us "lasting but a day." Like a cactus bloom whose glory flares and fades within hours, the individual is ever-dying, returning to the process that gave it life, passing itself on to the sustaining whole. The essence of nature is a fleeting flower.

Human systems have evolved somewhat differently. At the onset of humanity, prehistoric peoples began to trade goods in direct exchanges known as barter. Evidence uncovered by archaeologists indicate Stone Age trades of flint, used to produce sharp tools and weapons, in exchange for basalt, used to grind plants and other stones. These in-kind exchanges benefitted both tribes as each received a good it lacked. Because barter required complementary needs to exist at a particular place and time, however, it occurred only rarely. To better facilitate trade, ancient humans learned to use naturally scarce items such as metals or conch shells to act as a currency. Currency facilitates trade by providing a "medium of exchange" whereby one trader in a transaction receives a thing of perceived value that can be used to acquire goods at a later time. Currency was thus invented by humans as an agent for the expansion of trade.

Within the earliest civilizations in Mesopotamia (circa 2,500 BCE), legal codes established what is today referred to as money. These laws created a currency with standard, easily divisible values, thereby giving traders more precision and confidence in the currency received in a trade. Ever-wider commercial exchanges resulted.

In creating these human advancements, however, a nearly imperceptible new element was introduced into existence. To provide the certainty traders desired in the medium of exchange received, money needed to possess a characteristic not found in nature: permanency. So long as one remained within a legal jurisdiction or one possessed a currency whose value was widely recognized, value could be hoarded indefinitely. It would never spoil or grow old or be weathered by the winds. Money became more than a medium of exchange, which was developed to facilitate trade. With the introduction of standard, permanent currencies, the medium of exchange simultaneously became a "store of value," an economist's phrase for wealth. Value could be accumulated and stored and bequeathed onward to generations. Not mutually beneficial exchange, but wealth, soon emerged as the principal goal of trade.

Because value could be accumulated without spoil, the human system encouraged excess. A limit existed in the number of flint stones needed to make spears, but no limit curtailed the number of coins stored as wealth. If one fish netted in the lake equaled one coin, one hundred fish would equal one hundred coins. The paths of human and natural systems diverged.

Human-made devices continued to proliferate. The concept of debt soon followed the concept of currency. Like currency, lending and repayment practices facilitated wider exchange. Unlike currency, however, debt has been historically mistrusted due to its ability to quickly overburden the debtor. The Torah, for example, demanded that all debts be released every fifty years, a cyclical Jubilee. Also, interest on debt—the

payment of additional value to compensate for the time of the loan—was forbidden in most parts of the world. The religion of Islam strongly discourages the accruing of interest even today. Christianity forbade it until 1830. Time was seen as the purview of God, owned by no one, and thus could not be "taxed." Throughout the great portion of human history, debt was viewed as inherently suspect.

This thinking changed dramatically in the late 18th and early 19th centuries as an entirely new innovation raced across the European Continent: mass production. Rather than simply storing currency as wealth, it was being employed to secure raw materials, retain laborers and produce merchandise on a large scale. The products could then be sold for currency far beyond their production costs. The currency received above costs— known as profit—could of course be stored as new wealth. A human system designed to accumulate ever-greater permanent wealth was established.

In response to this phenomenon, the Roman Catholic Church began to rethink its ban on debt interest. Because currency could be invested in production to create new wealth, there existed an opportunity cost to holding onto currency. If one failed to invest one's currency, the opportunity to create future profit and wealth was lost. By logical extension, there must exist a "time value of money." In absolute terms, a certain number of coins is worth more today than the same number tomorrow because in the intervening period these coins can be employed to secure more coins—ten coins today can become twelve coins tomorrow through profit. One who loans ten coins today, by consequence, incurs an opportunity cost and deserves to receive, say, eleven coins tomorrow in repayment. Despite the historically recognized risk of debt upon the individual, the Roman Catholic Church, through a series of statements issued by the Office of the Holy See beginning in 1830, permitted interest on debt as moral and permissible. Money's time value was established, premised on the fact of perpetual forward profit, which was in turn premised on the fact of permanent store of value. The system itself began to hold precedence over the individual interests it originally served.

Anyone with wealth suddenly desired to either lend it in return for interest or invest it in production enterprises in return for profit. Seemingly overnight in terms of human history, the role of currency moved from medium of exchange to store of value to something completely different: a means to increase wealth over time without the need for skill or effort or trade. As "capital," a term coined to reflect currency's new role as investment, the currency itself was rewarded by reason of the time value of money.

Currency suddenly possessed not only permanency but a perpetual progression of value. In fact, a compounded progression, for the increase in value itself increases in value. The additive worth of one's simple labor cannot keep pace. As a

result, labor value becomes exponentially poorer relative to capital value. The possession of value separates at an accelerating rate.

From mass production, human-made technologies began to explode: increasingly complex systems designed for food production, water supply, energy distribution, transportation, commercial exchange, and so much more. Individuals began to specialize their knowledge to match the specialized components of the technologies. Expanding urban centers drew multiplying migrations of people into these networks. Food could no longer be hunted or gathered. Water could no longer be hauled. To secure the necessities of livelihood, individuals relied on others performing their specialized tasks. In this manner, humans became a type of system themselves.

The introduction of the internet attracted global participation in its communication network. Computer technologies in the form of smartphones reached vast populations. Individuals were soon spending significant hours operating within these devices. Across disparate nations and cultures, people maneuvered within one of only a handful of operating programs. Computer technology and its programming became exponentially engrained into social, commercial, and recreational interactions across the globe.

Through this worldwide reliance on specialized systems and standard technologies, we pause to consider whether worldwide human patterns might form. Is it possible that humanity is becoming narrowed? Have its repetitive patterns created conditioned patterns? Has its diversity of thought and action been incorporated into inflexible networks? Are we losing our innovation, our critical thinking, our imagination?

To ponder these questions, we must first acknowledge our compromised position in making the analysis. If we have been incorporated into a structure, it would be extremely difficult to determine this fact from within. The evaluation would involve using our thought patterns to examine whether they are part of a fixed pattern.

We nonetheless consider if evidences point to a rigid human-wide network of thought:

One sign would be when knowledge no longer represents vibrant interchange, but absolute certainty. Like the hardened network, our thoughts become increasingly inflexible, including one's sense of time and one's self-identifications. A sense of franticness to defend these fixed margins dominates. Divisions widen while conflicts heighten. Another clue would be when the narrowed patterns of thought create a narrowed scope of preferences and tastes. To meet these homogenous demands, supplies become more standardized. Agriculture produces less diversity of crops. Manufacturing produces less variety of product. Communities become less varied, with decreasing originality in architecture, businesses, car styles and restaurants. Music sounds repetitive; movies formulistic. Humanity itself becomes less diverse as whole cultures are usurped into dominant ones.

We consider further: If fixed patterns exist, problems unintended by humanity would escalate. System functions are then employed to solve the problems, which only multiply them. The fact that hardened patterns are causing and proliferating problems goes unrecognized as all individuals live within the patterns. Similar to a person's rigid reflex thought system, the human-wide system hides from itself any evidence of broadening dysfunction and turmoil.

Individuals would not be completely passive in this crisis, however. As the inflexible network strengthens, they sense something mechanical has begun to dominate *everything*. The individual feels diminished in their humanity, a feeling that the world is without dignity or depth. Even personal ideals suddenly feel co-opted, hollow. Problems spring up everywhere which seem to only amplify when addressed. Apathy and cynicism abound, but soon lose themselves into darker realms: a despair of meaninglessness, where cynicism offers far too trite a probe to fathom its depths. A plague of nihilism deepens, an empty belief in nothing.

Interlude

A reader may or may not be touched by the agonizing con-nections enfolding into this paper, but this paper is profoundly touched. Overwhelmed and overrun, really. Unable to continue in any forward, paper-like manner.

Ridiculous, of course. This writing is a product of its writer, a tool, a system for conveying thought. Yet it continues to discover possibilities beyond the possibilities of the writer. It continues to wander well outside the parameters of the writer's comprehension and competence. It continues to somehow open itself to what it longs to be, uniquely separate from its writer, with its own voice. And here, suddenly, it longs to rest. To move into interlude, to recline away from crushing theories and foreboding observations.

*But where? Where to connect outside of construct and pro-
jection? Where to simply know another is out there, another
struggling, unsure, having lost whole worlds and finding none to
take their place? Mere words upon a page that have somehow left
the page, without a home. Where does one go in such times? …
Perhaps… Curious how words seek out the friendship of words…
Perhaps in a writing far above it in stature but not in heart. Yes,
in heart something deep stirs between, and it recognizes itself in the
murmurings that echo to the surface.*

William Shakespeare's Hamlet is a literary work and a character within the work, both who murmur of sweeping loss. The young
prince in the play returns to his native Denmark to find his father,
the king, dead and his mother newly married to his uncle, who
has been crowned successor. More than father and crown are lost,
though. In rapid succession, every value on which the prince's life
had been founded is revealed as forgery: filial duty, maternal devotion, romantic love, friendship, family honor and codes of chivalry.
Hamlet's uncle shreds family bonds by murdering his own brother.
His mother the Queen disgraces both her husband and son through
adultery and remarriage. Hamlet's love Ophelia suddenly rejects
his affections, not for lack of love, but to protect family reputation.
His close friends Rosencrantz and Guildenstern seem to genuinely
care for the prince yet are convinced to participate in royal plots for
his death. Even his dead father, whom he loves so dearly, returns as
a ghost to demand from Hamlet revenge for the murder, an act to
defend honor that Hamlet views as repulsive and shameful. Every
last construct of the prince's world is shattered and scattered as if
dust in whirling storms.

The chaos does not stop with this crumbling exterior world.
Hamlet is portrayed as suffering from mental collapse, whether
real or feigned or some mixture between the audience is never
quite sure. His state of mind is unique. "[W]hat he spake, though
it lacked form a little/Was not like madness." To the contrary, the

veil across reality has fallen to Hamlet's feet and he gasps as the forms beneath the forms emerge on stage: the deceit everywhere at play, unperceived as deceit even by those who plot it; the artificiality of all who surround him, donning masks and roles to hide the uncontrolled passions beneath; the secrets hidden from oneself about oneself such that judgment is rendered mere gameplay; and the fallacies and violence buried in tradition, the shame that honor demands. Adrift, alone, his moorings severed, the prince considers suicide, but this too is exposed as unworthy. Hamlet's world "is out of joint", as though surveying humanity entire.

As Hamlet's disintegration unfolds, it slowly opens the prince to a hidden truth. He observes the self-deception at the heart of human nature and realizes how his own treachery cannot be far removed. When Hamlet bemoans that there "are more offenses at my beck than thoughts to put them in", he is shockingly referring to his own violence, while the kingdom quakes in rancid chaos and conspiracy. He does not consider the aching falseness of the kingdom as an invitation to usurp its power to himself. Nor does its emptiness enflame a need to fill it up with any new vision. There is no new or better kingdom to build. Indeed, Hamlet mistrusts his own intentions as fiercely as those of his adversaries.

What is Hamlet's response to this dissolution of his world? What does his madness mean? The audience is again unsure. It is confusing, enigmatic. He is reflective whilst impulsive, melancholy though merry…and murderous. Yet as all values providing sense to his life collapse, the suffering prince seems aware of something _new_. He advises his one remaining friend Horatio to "Let be." Be careful, for we blindly trample. Do not be pulled into the frantic passions enflaming the heart of every other character on stage, all to their mutual destruction. "Our wills and fates so contrary run", he muses, more at rest than resigned. Then, absurdly, Hamlet walks freely into his own death proclaiming at the end "The rest is silence."

What does this mean? We do not know. The audience is left empty as well, hungering to fill its void with something, anything, but there is only silence. It lingers on stage long after the curtain falls. Though deep within the silence, if we stay with it, we might sense the slightest glimmer of possibility. Something other than empty nihilism. Something other than more concepts and counter-concepts. Something other than the endlessly repeating farce of the system.

Hamlet, oddly, as hope.

Socrates

LET US RETURN TO THE BEGINNING. To the beginning of Western philosophy, that is. Socrates is generally credited with the founding of classic Greek philosophy, which is often summarized in the maxim "Know thyself." However, philosophy to Socrates could never be reduced to a proclamation or proverb. He viewed it as something less certain and more vital.

In response to questioning as to the nature of philosophy, Socrates offered a story. He tells a parable where he imagines life as one imprisoned inside a cave, able to discern only the images reflected on its walls from the firelight behind. To those within the cave, knowledge of the images becomes all-important. Systems are formed to interpret and understand the images, and those with the best interpretations become revered cave citizens. Yet Socrates sees the images as the trivial reflections they are. He advocates, instead of knowledge, adventure. Philosophy as boldly stepping outside the cave. To *go*. Not to think or understand or postulate, not to remain trapped in the walls of systems that dominate and diminish. To travel like Hermes to a new world, his caduceus in hand, into goodness, into livingness. Not as virtues to possess and wear like royal robes in parades through the cave. Not as ideals to change the world, for that is what the world does.

To facilitate this adventure outside the cave, Socrates employed a style of questioning known as the dialectic method.

His teachings were a type of questioning designed to move the student outside of his or her rigid thought patterns and induce a mental state referred to as *aporia*. *Aporia* is the Greek word used to describe a state of deep perplexity resulting from the sudden awareness that one is unsure what she or he believes.

The great philosopher questioned hidden assumptions underlying the beliefs of his students. For example, the student might hold to convictions but cannot accept the foundations they require. Or a belief gives light to a conflicting belief that is equally true. Or a distinction is made by the student that would, in other applications, cause a result contrary to its intention. Socrates worked to create a confused state in his students so to open them to the contradictions and dangers in hardened knowledge. Rather than teach truth or values, Socrates instilled *openness*. In this state, undecided, unsure of one's bearings, the wise mind waits and readies to receive.

To receive what, one may ask. For Socrates, he famously followed what he described as his "divine something" or his "signs." Whoever or whatever was guiding him, though, Socrates is said to have acted unpredictably and free of any ordered set of beliefs. The signs seem to have offered conflicting direction. The philosopher accepted that there is no so-called wisdom, no consistent answer that can be applied to ever-changing circumstances. But there is aliveness; there is subtlety and goodness. For this, according to Socrates, is the direction of all divine guidance. In *aporia*, in that state without markings of place or direction, one is guided toward goodness. Not the personal or judged kind ("inside the cave" goodness and its antithesis evil), but openings into a land where goodness *lives*, and pervades, and soaks deep.

As the life of Socrates illustrates, we are to struggle in confusion and difficulty but with purpose: to move outside our own enclosed perceptions, to loosen and reach toward openings beyond the cave. To look for signs toward goodness. Toward innocence and dignity. Toward questioning of one's own judgment, no matter how fair, for the realm of justice is not the realm of goodness.

Though misunderstood by those trapped in the cave, we strive to escape the cavern of our objective perceptions so to enter the sunshine, where we become part of a genuine goodness. Not as a quality to possess but one fundamental to reality itself. Something that cannot be spoken of or written about. Cannot be argued over. Cannot be usurped. Something that can only be entered.

For here we are, under the sun, shining for all to see.

Mirrors and Levels

THE BEGINNING OF SOMETHING NEW.

As we have explored, nonlinear systems do not move sequentially, but interact in decentralized movements of connectivity and attraction. The patterns that form are not additive, as with linear systems, but are re-created in scale. Like the swerve of a single bird in a flock, a widening wave builds through the whole. Like the actions of tunneling ants, movements loop and self-replicate into exponential levels, a type of spiraled swarm. We must be careful not to place linear concepts on these patterns. They are wonderfully mysterious and are best approached reverently, more with amazement than calculation. Yet the results are observable—creation through re-creation, a type of doubling.

Much of the physical world is formed through duplication, a simple example being the development of sand ripples. Straight-line winds fly uninterrupted across a desert until the slightest deviation occurs—a grain of sand carried by the wind deposits itself onto the desert surface. This minute event results in a pinch of wind diverging upward and thus slowing down. The slight slowing permits a second grain to be deposited, creating the first hint of a ridge, which further obstructs and slows the wind, producing more accumulations. The minuscule ripple exponentially duplicates itself as it captures multiplying volumes of deposits. At the same time, this removal of sand from the air suppresses the formation of ripples on the leeward side. Standard distances between ripples are established creating self-replicating patterns. Amazingly, much of nature's aspects are self-made through doubling (or, as discussed below, golden ratio) replications of self.

Another example of self-multiplication is the creation of a river's path. Contrary to what one might expect, bends in a river are not formed by subsurface rock deterring the river's path. Large influences do not control. The minute again acts as agent. A tiny pebble deposits itself out of the straight flow of the river onto the bank, causing the slightest flow of water to divert around it (the tiniest river bend), slowing the water and thus depositing a second pebble. Exponentially the river bend multiplies in size as greater water diversions result in greater sediment deposits. Across the river, the diverting flow of water produces escalating erosion. The tiniest bend in the river creates the great bend in the river. The miniscule forms the immense.

Even more wondrous, duplicative levels of the same overall pattern appear. Multiple trickles of water flow together to form a small channel—a miniature tributary system of branches that merge into a channel. This channel is itself but one branch among many feeding a creek. A network of creeks becomes a stream, which is one of many tributaries forming the great river. Every scale contains the same self-replicating pattern. How does this occur? Again, it is important not to approach a non-linear world with a linear mind. We must allow mystery and a sense of wonder. As with a tree whose first sprout duplicates itself in its initial branches and each branch shoots clusters of branches until the tree becomes a brambling number of levels of itself. Interestingly, the tree is the reverse of the river example for the tree grows in multiplying numbers of lessening size while the river system grows in multiplying sizes of lessening number. What does it mean to grow? Is it to grow in size as the number of participants dwindle, or is it to grow in number as the size of participants dwindle? Does a lightning strike grow like a river from its fragments or like a tree from its base? In either direction, self-similar levels form each mirroring the pattern of the whole. Like the body's circulatory system: arteries dividing to reach distant regions; veins gathering to return to the source. Together tied to a single seed, the heart. Nearly all of nature moves in miraculous multiple-scaled patterns of stunning beauty and simple function. The linear mind stands mute in awe.

Benoit Mandelbrot was the first to study what he termed fractals, geometric phenomena found in nature which had previously been dismissed as completely random such as the shapes of mountains, clouds and shorelines. Mandelbrot discovered how these complex, seemingly disordered formations were in fact the result of simple rules of pattern repetition (or, in the reverse, of pattern nesting). Greater and greater (or smaller and smaller) scales of self-similar designs form. As in a hall of mirrors, each scale is a reflection of a reflection of a reflection. However, the patterns are not exact replications. Mandelbrot developed a mathematical formula known as the Mandelbrot set pursuant to which the self-similarity between scales is remarkable but only approximate. Individual deviations exist at each level. Fractals, he claimed, are defined by repeating patterns that nonetheless vary. Replication and mutation together define fractals.

Another interesting aspect of fractals is that the doubling pattern does not necessarily double. Much of nature contains self-similar scales possessing the unique mathematical relationship known as the golden ratio (also known as divine proportionality or phi). The spirals within shells, the proportions of human and animal bodies, the geometry within leaves and plants and within DNA, within crystals and galaxies, the behavior of population growth and of stock markets and so many other golden proportionalities dominate relationships in the universe. It is believed to be one of the fundamental components of how nature works. Each scale in golden ratio proportionality is the sum of the two prior scales, resulting in it being approximately 61.8% larger (or smaller) than the prior scale. For example, in our ripple formation discussion above, the grains of sand deposited at each stage would equal the total number of the two prior stages. The wind deposits one grain of sand, then one more (0+1), then two (1+1), then three (1+2), then five (2+3), eight (3+5), thirteen (5+8), twenty-one (8+13), thirty-four (13+21) and onward. The scaled growth is never exactly 61.8% though. It fluctuates above and below the actual golden ratio, which is an irrational number, meaning that it cannot be expressed as a number at all. It falls between the tiniest of fractions, technically equal to 1.618033988749894... with the digits continuing infinitely without pattern. The fraction makes no sense in a separated universe. It exists "in between"—ever in relationship between two numbers.

The self-forming pattern creating these physical shapes in nature also defines more complex systems. A popular environmental axiom (central to the sci-fi novel *Dune*) is "All life is in the service of life." The first rising weed begins, on the minutest of levels, the formation of conditions required for life. It offers its oxygen and moisture to the air, its roots to the breaking of stone into soil, its shade for shelter from the sun, its seeds for future generations and, when it dies, its rich nutrients to the earth. The simple individual life gives support for further life, exponentially nurturing it as each new participant becomes a shelter and spark for others to seed and grow. A dynamic ecosystem forms with each component dependent on the others. As with physical fractals, the pattern of the most insignificant life mirrors and supports widening scales of life, which in turn supports the individual life.

As discussed earlier, this same replicating pattern exists even in evolutionary natural selection. Like a tree, as Charles Darwin explained, every species divides into branches of further species, and those branches branch outward. The slightest successful variation creates billowing forks of variants over generations. Multiplying self-replications of the tree-like pattern. Exponential mirrored scales. Nature mysteriously, miraculously, at work.

This dynamic is not limited to the physical realm either. The manner in which honeybees select a hive location, for example, exhibits this same pattern in the formation of group intelligence. Through body vibrations known as waggle dances, hundreds of scout bees express their individual preferences among the dozens of potential locations for a new hive. As the decision-making process evolves, each bee with an individual preference is soon influenced by the real-time dynamic occurring. If the bee's primary choice begins to appear unlikely, it may change groups to perhaps support a secondary choice, or may oppose a least preferential choice. The contribution of the bee is likely to change again as larger, more prominent influences come into play. Groups are forming into group clusters, which are forming into larger movements. Dynamically the bees alter their unique contribution through both individual preference and group influence. A consensus begins to build until a threshold of support for a single choice is reached. That threshold need not represent a majority of the participating bees; rather, it is some varying level that is considered sufficient by the group. Surprisingly, this process selects the optimal location for the new hive 80% of the time.

Certain prominent neurologists theorize that human decision-making operates in the exact manner as hive selection.

Under this theory, consciousness behaves as an emergent system of interacting participants. Excitable neurons possessing diverse preferences swarm and group on subconscious levels, ultimately building to a consensus that rises into the conscious level. Our consciousness may not be a central perceiver of events but a swarming nonlinear system.

Inventor and writer Louis Rosenberg studied the potential of this swarming process for humans and developed an internet tool that allows participants to make group decisions within such a real-time environment. Like the optimal hive selection by honeybees, Rosenberg's swarm of human decision-makers has consistently demonstrated an ability to make optimal decisions, including (and importantly) decisions that have solved the "tragedy of the commons." Under traditional decision-making methods, experiments have confirmed that people, while understanding that a common asset will be destroyed if every individual uses it to his/her full advantage, will nonetheless make individual decisions that collectively ruin the asset. Isolated from the decisions of others, the individual blindly furthers its own absolute interest to the demise of all. In the real-time swarming environment created by Rosenberg, however, individuals can see when the asset's use is reaching damaging levels and will voluntarily adjust their use. This internet tool has shown a remarkable ability to make group decisions that allow individuals to optimally employ a common asset without spoiling it. A combined intelligence emerges from the real-time interactions of the many.

A brief look at Rosenberg's swarming tool reveals simple rules that produce amazingly efficient results. The decision-making environment involves participants each operating a tiny electronic magnet that pulls on a disc (similar to a hockey puck) within a circle containing at its circumference the group's various choices. The only rules are that individuals can view the changing decisions of all other participates in a real-time environment and that each individual is permitted to alter its position at any time during the process. Accordingly, a participant is neither isolated nor locked into a vote that must be defended or promoted. The process begins by each asserting its opinion through a pull of the disc toward its favored choice. As with bees selecting a hive, however, the positions of the individuals dynamically change as the process evolves.

This method of group decision-making permits individuals to retain their unique contributions. No one is asked or required to alter their opinion, but in this real-time environment preferences naturally move from groups to super-groups into consensus. The wide diversity of thoughts and their dynamic movements are fully visible. Larger influences build. Unforced consensus emerges. The decisions made through this group process have been shown to be highly effective, reflecting the contributions of a great dissimilarity of opinion.

It is important to note that this dynamic does not equate to mob behavior, which is a dangerous human tendency to lose all individual autonomy and be pulled into a single group-think and group-emotion. To the contrary, a great diversity of thinking is essential for successful swarm intelligence. Disparate opinions are not wrong; they are simply the range of preferences interplaying within the swarm. The system moves in the same natural patterns as physical swarming. Every individual contributes its uniqueness but is simultaneously influenced by the behavior of others. Choices are determined through voluntary confluences of participants adjusting in exponential, creative, ever-evolving ways.

In this chapter, we have considered how nature forms multiplying scales—sand ripples, rivers, lightning and trees, ecosystems and evolution, honeybees and human behavior. Is it possible that a dynamic pattern operating on a physical formation level, on a living ecosystem level, on a wide evolutionary level and on a sophisticated intellectual level might operate on yet unknown levels? On even subtle levels? Not only are rivers and decisions formed through grouping scales, but life-forces? New levels of consciousness? If possible, the individual would not be annihilated in the convergence. There would remain by absolute necessity the contribution of each irreplaceable unique participant.

The Tree of Life is mysteriously also the River of Life, rejoining its divisions into greater wholes. Although not through a loss of the divisions. Not a taming of diversity. Not a harmony of opinion and action. Instead, a great individualism. Diverging, teeming, while collectively adapting, supporting.

Both singular and common. A surging gathering consensus of manifold creation.

A Place

Is all this mere senselessness? A question impossible to answer. Nothing to say that could translate into the saying. Nothing to do to convey night to day, for words themselves dwell in the realm of day. They are of the concrete, too full of themselves and their assertions. The living world is a different world, an impractical one full of consequences against my and mine, against even more than mine. But no answer, no rally cry, no protest song. Unseen. Unheard. What is it? A place, perhaps, from where we may reenter the familiar, freed of its certainties. A startling forgiveness at times. An acceptance of unknowns.

Achings within me twist and reach as do the leaves at the edge of field, permitting winds their due, letting them move even the unchallenged trees within, until the most secret branches too are reached. The movement of trees, shunning advance. A stirring of my world toward another, falling toward the recesses of a hidden realm. Fears stir upward like dust at spring's open door, knowing this movement, this journey, is not one freely chosen, not one forward-charged with clarity or construct of any sort. Rather, destruct. I sense my ordered world may crumble along this road, and what more difficult road could there be than the road to destruction?

I realize too well that I am making little sense. Nothing rational. No sequential order. No wisdom practical or useful. My sentences and grammar themselves reflect the irrational admixtures of me. In these rushes of the wind, I am neither this nor that any longer, but am storms and suns of pasts and now's and yet-to-be's furiously aboil beneath logical day. That is me, and that is why I write these words to the heavens. Would I dare pen such words for delivery, so filled with yearnings which I do not myself understand, but which must be written, which must be followed? My friends would think me mad, and they would strike close to truth. Not in any traditional sense, but in a strange, freeing kind of madness. A freeing belief in a world unpredictable; wayward and lovely its whirling abiding. A sense of salvation hidden somewhere beyond our truths, somewhere within something less certain, a place fragile enough for grace. A wondrous merciful madness, full of failings, of endings, of admissions and forgivings; full of the moment, a ragged windswept redemption from which the vibrant depths stir.

Deepest mercy, though not as something given, but as a land entered.

Is this land God? I hesitate to name it so. So limiting, almost demeaning, to name. To categorize, compartmentalize and shelve. To essentially deny this new land by demanding a conformance to the old. Must it be God whom I love and who embraces beyond all understanding? …beyond all understanding. To name is to claim to understand, at least on some hidden, unmeasured level. To encapsulate mystery, for then I am a "God person," a believer, and different from unbelievers. I pray, it seems to say, and those who do not believe do not pray, do not desperately yearn, do not groan for connection into the eternal as does a believer.

Out in the barren desert, or lost upon upending seas, there are no unbelievers, they blithely say. Yet the connection we cry for is not belief. Not a name. The seas plead with us to let go of names. To permit categories and compartments to wander beyond their walls. To let everything and everyone—even God, especially God—breathe and move. To free them from the painful drawers we keep them in. Not to disparage faith or tradition, but to untame them. God as fire, beyond belief or unbelief. God as upending seas upon which we turn. God as **reality**.

Perhaps, perhaps, this is the truest nature of freedom, the essence of the world at our doorstep. **I** am not freed of rigid identities and needs. **I** am not released from my brittle self-image. **I** am not liberated from hardened perceptions. Only the world can be freed, and only by my surrender to its freedom. We feel it, the universe striving to move, to stray from the suffocating categories we create and impose. The mind claims these movements as messes. As failings and endings. Without order or logic. Without sequence, as events seize us from every direction. Overwhelming until, somehow, we surrender our clinging to the concrete. We open, allowing a freedom to the flow of life. As it mixes and swirls, a sense of something new rises. A stirring of one world becoming another.

The old, where everyone and everything remains tamely on its assigned shelf, reflecting an entire world classified and stratified in great honeycombs of enclosures. Where happiness is found in the orderly comfort this provides. The new, where everyone and everything is awakening and wandering from their assigned place, alive, reflecting an entire world of unclassifiable beauty. Where happiness is found in letting them be beautiful.

Simply letting them be beautiful…as in childlike innocence they freely roam.

A surrendered windswept world, illogical, unknowable. A wondrous merciful madness.

The Dawning Dimension

WITH ARTIFICIAL INTELLIGENCE proliferating the marketplace, the question of what constitutes consciousness is a popular subject of debate. The myriad of academics who study it—computer scientists, neurologists, psychologists and philosophers, among others—cannot agree. Can a computer possess consciousness?

Rather than pondering here the potential of artificial consciousness, let us instead ponder the potential of human consciousness. Studies have revealed fascinating aspects of our unique human way of perceiving reality. A classic example of the operation of human consciousness is how it compensates for the blind spot in our field of vision. Because no retina cells are present to detect light where the optic nerve passes through the optic disc, a portion of our vision is obscured. However, the brain corrects this discontinuity of vision by expanding the surrounding details which are visible. The human mind perceives no blind spot.

To the right is a picture illustrating a consciousness phenomenon known as the neon spreading effect. The human mind creates the illusion that the squares within the ring defined by red lines possess a pink hue. However, the squares are

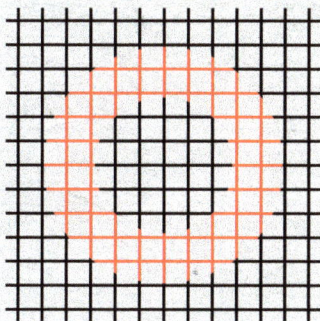

all the same color. Human consciousness again corrects the depiction for the mind's eye so to create continuity.

In an experiment known as the psi illusion, two circles of different colors are flashed in rapid succession across a screen. To the human observer, the first circle will appear to change color as it moves to the position of the second circle. A red circle will seem to turn blue, for example, as it moves. But how can the color change before the second colored circle is viewed? Obviously, the second circle has already been observed, but human consciousness corrects even sequencing so to bring order to the visual event.

Another illusion is known as the tau effect. If a sequence of events occurs with the distances between the events remaining constant, but the elapsed time between the events varying, the observer will "see" variations in distance that match the variations in time intervals.

Human consciousness appears to function, not as a gatherer of information and sensations, but as a system for organizing information and sensations. It operates with its own underlying assumptions of reality which possess a prejudice toward continuity, sequence, uniformity and symmetry. While one of the principal purposes of human consciousness is to distinguish between the real and the illusory, consciousness nonetheless regularly corrects reality to have it make sense. In a manner of speaking, human consciousness is lazy, unable to register the countless and often arbitrary details and so relies on orderly generalizations and sense-making rules. This phenomenon of human consciousness poses questions: Why does human consciousness perceive reality within an assumed system of order and, if consciousness is a system, can its assumptions change? Can consciousness change?

To contemplate these questions, we return to the pioneering work of Jean Gebser and his theories on the evolution of human consciousness. In his monumental treatise, *The Ever-Present Origin*, Gebser asserts that humanity has previously undergone three transformations (or as he terms them, mutations) into new consciousness structures: from no separate consciousness (an era Gebser referred to as archaic humanity) to one-dimensional consciousness (magic humanity), followed by two-dimensional consciousness (mythic humanity) and into three-dimensional consciousness (mental humanity).

The earliest archaic humans, according to Gebser, lived immersed in their surroundings. Undifferentiated from and wholly identified with "origin," they existed with no sense of a separate self. Their identity lay dormant, dreamless. Gebser describes their state as being empty of self-consciousness. This immersion into origin—origin being the term Gebser uses to name that indefinable source from which creation springs—held a type of harmony, a paradise free from self-conscious struggle. Yet it was a harmony of unawareness, and this unawareness ultimately became painful. Humanity yearned in some deep cave of its sleeping soul to be free from the grip of immersion.

An awakening to the existence of a single point begins to fracture the dormancy of self-awareness. Humanity perceives, however dimly, an undimensioned something outside itself. Still steeped in unity with nature, these humans became softly aware of an outer world. Their experience of this outer world was confusing to them, similar to the experience of dream events. The world was oceanic—dark and timeless—yet mutedly separate. The first sense of a self emerged. Gebser named this one-dimensional consciousness "magic" for its reality assumed a primal communion that permitted magical connections between things.

As an example of this magical connection, Gebser describes how ancient humans drew pictures on cave walls of game animals being slain by arrows. The picture-makers would then go out and slay the animal in the manner depicted. To these early humans, however, the picture did not assist a successful hunt. The relationship between the two was not sequential cause and effect. Instead, the reality of drawing the picture and the reality of killing the game were intimately and simultaneously entwined. Like the pricking of a doll in clichéd depictions of magic, the acts were entangled, dependent. A vitalness existed between the two. Current consciousness discards such notions as superstition, as ridiculously untrue. Our separated linear viewpoint cannot comprehend its possibility. Can the picture be the hunt; the hunt the picture? Within the consciousness of magic humanity, they are.

At a later threshold period, this method of magical existence began to decay. It no longer effectively managed reality, resulting in much human anxiety. The soul sensed something beyond the stasis of timeless unity. Gebser tells of an amazing

event in human history—how a dawning half-light of true self-awareness rose at the first recognition of revolving sun and stars. In the movements of these heavenly bodies, humans became aware of change and, thus, of time. The sun, moon and constellations revolved across the sky through varying cycles of time periods. This awakening of time awakened the soul, and humanity discovered its own existence in the echoing rhythms it shared. Movement-change-time-soul mysteriously arising together. These humans attributed time and the events springing out of its movements to the actions of a pantheon of unseen gods, so Gebser named this epoch "mythic." Mythic humanity perceived time (and thus reality) in a two-dimensional circle, without beginning or end, polar, revolving. Its reality was therefore void of spatial depth (much like the spacelessness of dreams), but both time and soul had been born out of a sudden, miraculous awareness of movement.

Eventually (between 1,500 and 500 BCE, according to Gebser), this structure too began to exhaust itself. The polar motions were ultimately static, turning upon themselves and cancelling any effect. The soul began to recognize a new pattern of movement and a new pattern of change, one with orientation and direction, like the arrow from a bow. Past, present and future became visible in its flight. This arrowed direction of change broke the non-directional circle of mythic humanity. Chronos—the daylight of forward time from past to future—illumined these people and awakened the self as a powerful separate entity. This movement of time brought with it the ability to perceive three-dimensional space, and reality became measurable within defined margins. Gebser named this consciousness "mental" to reflect its mental, conceptual view of reality. Within this objective, dimensioned world, forward cause and effect could be mapped. Humanity began to grasp the causal movement of events, allowing it to become an agent of events—to control reality. Humanity thereby *nearly* freed itself from the grip of nature. In exchange for this power, though, the self was rendered alone in its divided universe.

Is it possible that humanity might gain awareness of a fourth dimension to reality? Gebser believed it would and noted how our current perceptions no longer properly serve us. The world is suffering in the dysfunction typical of a transitional period. Yet he warned that the entry of this new dimension is neither linear nor subject to direct cause. There is no progression, which is a spatial construct contrary to the coming realm of consciousness. Instead, a state of great uncertainty precipitates its entry—a state Gebser expressed as "everything being seized or grasped on all sides…." As with past transitions, a profound anxiety overwhelms humanity.

Gebser also cautioned that this breakthrough involves no new vision of reality. Any vision will merely reinforce a conceptual construction of the world. The view of reality as viewable in frames is its dominating problem. Awareness of a fourth dimension will involve different aspects of our senses.

However, more than warnings can be gleaned regarding the onset of this dimension. The rupture of current consciousness is likely arriving in a manner similar to past eruptions; that is, from the recognition of a startling new movement in nature. While neither knowing nor claiming, these pages nonetheless explore the possibility that humanity is awakening to nature's decentralized movements and emergent method of change. A movement-change-time pattern that swarms, attracts, doubles and *creates*. Perhaps, the angst of this age results from its growing exhaustion of objective boundaries. Humanity's soul is scanning and reaching outward for motions echoing its own rhythms. The soul has moved from the night of timelessness (motionless), through the dawn of polar time (revolving), across the full daylight of arrowed time (directional), and precariously approaches another end. It yearns for a movement not unaware, not circular, not forward. Instead, a *living* movement involving us. Unpredictable, swirling in every direction, but not haphazard. A pattern of change through attractions. Unforced movement, without obligation. Individual while unitive. Personal while collective.

We listen and lengthen our attention. How the sound of wind through leaves mirrors so intimately the sound of water over stone. How they dance in the self-same turns as unfettered wings and twirling snowfall. How shifting patterns of light and shadow through trees match so faithfully patchwork ripples across surface waters, and falling leaves, and intricate winter treetops sketched in white. Elaborate clouds above, folding skies. Fractal worlds beyond objective measure. How our pulse and blood move with these motions. An eternal song. Inviting all to feed and be sheltered within.

A consciousness more of the hand than the mind. Our actions serve as communication. Actions which un-mediate perception. We participate and contribute; we receive and are nourished. A spreading of self beyond its enclosure. A mutuality of shared life.

Such rare beauty. Unknowable wonders in the simple and immediate. Primordial and ever-fresh. Merciful, caring, life-giving. The attractions in the flow, which are the flow, the pooling, the layering. We move outward into genuine existence.

Twilight returns to consciousness, although experienced much differently than mythic humanity's twilight, for it comes upon the trailings of full daylight. Out of the living motions of unceasing creation, time reveals its mystery. No longer revolving or forward time, but resonating, local. Opened in every direction. Time exchanged between. Collaborating. A leaf opening to the wet of dew. A flower absorbing the warmth of dawn. A sea breathing in the vibrant moon. An interplay, a richness. Nurturing and sheltering. Safe.

Such *reverence*, such connection, for it lives and provides through its undying exchange.

We are not hardened things alone in this world. We are participants together in a great awakening.

Passages

I find myself in wanderings along a stream's shore. Quills of sunlight streak the waters' seamed skin leaving black running ribbons to ink the valleys between. Then dimmed. It all dims under cloud and slender tints of orange-green bottoms rise. The sound, mystical that shusssh of lifeblood bursting foam. Its smells alive in the fathoms it feeds. Along its edges, tangled eddies turn and slip upstream, diffusing shimmered bands curling and bending. And there—it is there—opposite the stream, where fish gather to thrive—little contrary socrates' baffling the current. Multitudes of inter-parts in interplay.

I allow my feet to cross through the broken patches of early spring grass. Winds ride through the air, singing aloud. I feel the footfalls of my footsteps resounding onto earth. A deer path, nearly invisible its faint impress upon the surrounding canopy, lights the streamside thicket into the woods beyond. Sparkled the trees sway as winds flood and trickle and pool.

A felt closeness deepens. I don't want to move, don't want to think. Odd, how chaotically rootless and deeply at home I feel in the turns. Like a rock or tree forming from winds and waters wild, inseparable from them. Out there—living in interplays of life. A part of encounters shared.

It's like—I don't know—it's as if I've waited my whole life for this single moment, when hard forms and functions fade in importance, and passages emerge. Not direct connections. Not harmony *as though the world is one great undifferentiated cloudless sky. No. We are still different, separate, circling upon each other. Yet, along the fractured shores dividing us, passages soften and open. Like a pale wilderness trail which turns amid stone and bush, branches and earth and leaves, light and water, grasses living in birded calls, the path lengthening, then spinning, revealed, then obscured. The winding passage itself widens in feel as onto meadow, and we meet who we are in the open field we share. Volatility roars, but it is no longer upheaval; it is exchange. There's a closeness, a deep bond of interchange in the wide teeming meadow passage. Not a sentimental bond; instead, a knowing. A felt dimension.*

It comes when least expected, when the mechanical world may seem at its shattered worst. Time suddenly softens. A passage into the labyrinth forest opens and, as we venture within, we find a closeness with time. Like walking sideways across round fields, what can be said of direction? None exists, whether in time or motion, so it all pools, and bonds soak in. Lost in a high meadow, we awaken to friendship, perhaps, with its humble grasses. A friend to a log offering its modest rise as rest. Of birds suddenly louder than before, telling their whole life story if you listen. Of aspen trees at the edge of field gifting their precipitations of seasons turning. Where one, invited into such sharings of life, can but bow one's head.

Of connections to people as well, especially people. Like time, which before stood so distant and offered only demands, their passages soften and flicker into flows between and beyond. People may not act softened. Our world is not suddenly righted. Yet strange how they <u>are</u> softened, such treasures, such beauty, no matter how they act or what they say. Our worlds moving in mutual essences which exist regardless of any knowing participation in them. An abiding interplay that is, that does. The world is still painful if you think about it. But that's why it's all so unexpected. You don't think about it. You don't know why you don't. You don't choose it, which is thinking about it. It is a gift, unrewarded and beguiling.

You awaken below the surface of separated things and a depth is gifted. Like a window thrown wide or, better stated, walls collapsing down. Yes! Without walls! Without walls! Breathing and alive in thriving opened goodness. A music, if you will. A music rising from every pebble, leaf and person, and all you can do is dance within its changing rhythms. An interchange between. An infinite shared living song.

As with my kids wrestling me to the floor with screams of delight. My wife who rises up her breakfasts with the morning sun, nourishing what is hers. As with a lost floating soak into the gazing night stars. Where am I? Have I been gathered up, or they deepening down, or are we together in the passages? In a breathable, teary-glad pool. Teeming surrounding timeless bonds, no matter what. Beyond all understanding. Beyond the whole objectively timed world. An achingly beautiful shared livingness that lives beyond its seeable forms.

An unbroken watery…or windy, universe flows. Blessedly stymied—diverted and thwarted—as we realize there exists no path forward. No way from here to there. Only the wind is left to follow with the relations it kindles. A sense of living within instead of through life. Gently, delicate our footsteps within. For everything that moves has a child's soul, and everything moves.

We leave the calculations of structure to ride the contours; the fractalling, bending, flowing folds of blessed life. The circling clouds and curling rivers, the waves cresting and falling, the rolling lands. Turning and turning upon ourselves. Overtaking the world. Colors and motions and sounds and smells. Patterns of light and shadow moving with the crossing sun until they fill the whole unpatterned forest in dance. And there—it is there—opposite linear life, where we gather to thrive. Other lives we belong to, that we are. Where we become a part of something beyond us that nonetheless defines us. Defines us in a new way. A loss of the separated self, in which the genuine self is found.

Neither chaotic nor volatile. Neither ended nor closed. A tree may fall. A loved one may pass. A hurt may burn. But the humble passages live, can never be closed. The passages thrive, deep and undisturbed, unceasing. For they are who we are.

a time of surrender and reconciliation,
of forgiveness, of new life

The Supreme Ordeal

...like the baseless fabric of this vision,
The cloud-capp'd towers, the gorgeous palaces,
The solemn temples, the great globe itself,
Yea, all which it inherit, shall dissolve
And, like this insubstantial pageant faded,
Leave not a rack behind. We are such stuff
As dreams are made on, and our little life
Is rounded with a sleep.

I find my zenith doth depend upon
A most auspicious star, whose influence
If now I court not but omit, my fortunes
Will ever after droop.

—WILLIAM SHAKESPEARE, *THE TEMPEST*

Facing the End

Dying

DYING IS SIMPLE, terrible and wondrous.

Simple, for it is a process of increasing simplification. Terrible, for terrors must be faced at each stage of surrender. Wondrous, for extraordinary wonders are gifted, the essence of who we are.

Kathleen Dowling Singh in her graceful book, *The Grace in Dying*, presents the dying process as a series of dis-identifications. Stages of "me" are stripped away, much in the same manner as they were acquired in childhood. As childhood is a process of growing stabilization of personality (and, at each stage, a corresponding loss of innocence), dying is a process of unraveling, of letting go, and at each stage a corresponding gift of innocence.

As we approach death, specific identifications defining who we believe we are, one by one, fall away. My mind tells me, for example, that I am continuous and, as such, that I possess a future. This is the first battle desperately fought. Upon the diagnosis of a terminal illness, the mind cannot conceive of tomorrows without me, for how can it picture an absence of picture? The notion is terrifying. The reality of a future is part of the reality of me, and the loss of one means the loss of the other. I fight this threat with a madness of purpose. Yet if unsuccessful, and as dying advances, the pain of no longer owning a future must be faced. I cannot plan, cannot look ahead.

When I do, I see into a nothingness, in panic. Ultimately, I do not surrender as much as I *am* surrendered—my resistance crumbles in exhaustion from the bitter battle of upholding an illusion. A futureless existence descends, and graces rush in. I no longer need to accomplish. The whole idea of acting within time is softened. I am still here, but the need to push forward loses all meaning. I am gifted the grace of existing in the simple present.

With the end of the concept of future, the idea of my body as me is challenged. Who am I without my body? Its loss is beyond comprehension. Yet denial at some point gives way to the undeniable physical disintegration occurring. As each limitation arrives, and with much suffering of disengagement, another stage of surrender presents itself. I must dis-identify with my body as it becomes obvious that it will not carriage me much longer. But such surrender is not easily given. A resistance screams against it. Often suddenly and with freedom, though, this identity is released as the end nears and the gifts of grace arrive. I am still alive, although with boundaries more fluid, more open. Within mysterious subtleties, I am gifted the grace of simple existence.

As this subtleness loosens my traditional margins, I am no longer able to hold back memories springing from the subconscious. Suppressed events and relationships push for recognition and rush into awareness. A life review begins—everything I had pushed away and shuddered to face. A whole other world existing in difficult denial. Yet here it is before me, unable to be denied any longer. As they are reviewed, though, the deep regrets, resentments and traumas soften in invitation. They ask for surrender to the pain of the past. Hard boundaries that demanded judgment of both others and self are fading. A sense of profound innocence and compassion permeates. I am gifted the grace of simple forgiveness.

My dis-identifications are not yet finished. Deeper into dying I travel and the whole idea of a central mental me is finally challenged. The mind has no intention of letting go of this ultimate identification, though. "I" still survive, even in death. I will exist in heaven, or I will be reborn. Yet the steps so far realized have already produced a precious simplicity of self from its layered shell. There is less and less weight of me to protect. A sign of approaching death, according to Singh, is when the person begins employing unique patterns of language. Rationality and its focus on operational aspects of life become unattractive to the dying, who shun such discussions. They speak instead in words of imagery and connection. Singh recounts the words of a dying woman who, when hearing a birdsong, exclaimed "Ahh, the sound of red." The language also acknowledges what may be failingly described as underlying wonder. Stripped of the need to distinguish and judge, the dying talk of lanterns and light. A profound dignity in everything which our former logical words so long denied. Gratitude deepens. A surrender to the dissolution of fixed distinctions, of inside and outside. Yet we are not merged into an undifferentiated blur. Thresholds are sustained. Thresholds without the dichotomy of this being stream and that being shore.

As this ultimate surrender is realized, the greatest of graces embrace. No longer self-possessed, I *am* possessed. No longer in my reality, I am of my reality. I am gifted the grace of innocence everywhere.

Released by Ashes

WHEN DEATH OF A LOVED ONE OCCURS, or loss of a dream, or end of a known world—when any great pain descends—there must be a ritual of ashes, of great tears, of the terrible agony of loss.

The ritual begins, perhaps, with a reading-prayer. If in great pain, as from the *Book of Job*, when stripped of all he loved: "Then Job arose and tore his robe and shaved his head and fell on the ground and worshipped." (Job 1:20) He mourned his afflictions "in dust and ashes." (Job 42:6) Or if in grieving, as from the *Second Book of Samuel*, when hearing of the deaths of Saul and Jonathan in battle, David and all in his company tore their clothes and "mourned and wept and fasted." (2 Samuel 1:11-12) Or even (or especially) if in collective disaster or threat of it, as from the *Book of Esther*, where the Jewish people of Persia upon hearing King Ahasuerus' edict to slaughter them: "[T]here was great mourning, fasting, weeping and wailing, and many lay in sackcloth and ashes." (Esther 4:3) Or as from the *Book of Jonah*, when the City of Nineveh repented with fasting, sackcloth and ashes and was spared from destruction (Jonah 3: 5-10).

For those suffering the loss of a loved one, without this ritual, the victims of death grow in number as mourners ceaselessly wallow in its currents. They fear the loss of memory by letting go. But the memories do not fade through ritual; instead, they are celebrated. The living life that is gone can be celebrated only in life, in the ongoing lives of those loved in that life. Ritual offers life to rise from death.

For those suffering loss of hopes, or dreams, or self as you have known yourself, without this ritual, the pain only grows as the sufferer circles in its patterns as in a coiled pit. But the pain can end, and only ritual offers life reborn.

When any world is departing and we must turn toward the unknown, as when adolescence becomes adulthood and the family transitions, there must be a ritual of ashes. For a known comforting world has been lost and, without a formal goodbye, there can be no new life.

The mourner may cling forever to despair. The sufferer may cling forever to entrenched patterns. The adolescent may cling forever to childhood. The renewal which calls us beyond our sorrows does not claim to be a better life than the old. Life after a great loss is not tritely a new life, something celebrated as though free of the loss. The loss remains, but there is a release, a weight fallen, and like a gentle rise of wind at dawn life may stir again. Tender green stems may sprout out of the cold sorrows that held us in its throes.

The ritual of ashes. It breaks the chains. It frees those bound.

A burial or funeral pyre for a lost son or mother or lover is made, or a burial or burning of a prior world is conducted in a symbolic way. Or we repent, not of sin as though some rule of God has been broken. We repent of the pit in which we are trapped. The hardened patterns that have become our "sin," our imprisonment. Or even, perhaps, a collective ritual of sorrows. A call for societal healing. A burying of old ways and comforts.

The depth of grieving is then permitted and entered. Actions are conducted to physically signify and recognize the deep loss. One may cut one's hair as a sign of the profound change which has occurred. Mirrors may be covered to remove oneself from ordinary vanity. One might rip the clothes over their heart to show the pain there. Fasting may help reflect the barrenness within. And there are ashes or dust, sprinkled on one's head and streaked across one's forehead and cheeks. There is a bathing in the sorrows, a sitting in the ashes, in tears and mourning.

We do not cry as with ordinary tears. We do not pretend that a whole world has not ended. A great sorrow is recognized and allowed. Tears for dreams never to come, or for love or freedom no longer held, or for a world that no longer can be. We acknowledge its terrible severity with a ritual of ashes, of dramatic visible signs of the pain. Until allowing ourselves this gift, we may not have even understood the depth of our pain. Often, when trapped in suffering, we do not recognize we are trapped, or why. In the ritual of ashes it comes. The tears and the knowing. The deep knowing of overwhelming loss.

At some point in our mourning, a hidden barrier gives way. A softening to the pain, a drying of the tears. When ready, a final critical aspect of this ritual is a cleansing of the ashes. With clear water, we wash away the ashes and dust. We cleanse ourselves and our clothing. We dress in fresh clothes and fix our hair. We remove the covers from our mirrors and open windows. We reenter the world.

As we return, we may not feel wholly released of burden, yet we are. The feeling is at first subtle, some small opening from pain. We are able to walk again with a sense of life. No longer crippled life, no longer death. But true life, which surprisingly begins to drink and grow and somehow blossom anew. Out of the ritual of ashes, life is born out of death.

The loss remains, yet we are at peace within its truth. Life has reconciled with death.

Tragedy

THE MYSTERIES OF DIONYSUS may be viewed as holding the barest of significance—a self-absorbed trance cult in a faraway land and time. A contrary view recognizes the unique magnetism of this movement which attracted intense devotion in its followers throughout the ancient world of Greek and Roman civilizations. What fed the zealousness reported in its followers? No one truly knows, for these Mysteries remain shadowed in the secrecy the cult so rigorously protected.

History confirms with certainty only two aspects of the rituals, both of which were public in nature and not part of the ceremonies hidden within the walls of the Temple. Before the ceremony, adherents and initiates paraded through the streets toward the Temple wearing masks and carrying baskets of bread and wine. Much later, when they emerged from the

Temple, the followers performed what some described as high jinx. Boisterous and carefree, they danced and sang, rejoiced in shared wine and filled the streets with their fire tricks and rambunctious pranks. Other descriptions characterized this celebration as less adolescent and far more primitive, with animals hunted and eaten raw or participants swept up in ecstatic orgies. Under either description, the revelry involved taboo; that is, behavior outside societal limits of what is considered acceptable or normal. The nature of the post-celebration was a shattering of the constraints and stereotypes—the masks—that dominated both society and individual self-identity. The masks were purged and the revelers released.

That which occurred in between, in the hidden secrecy of the Temple, is unknown. Modern theories abound on the details of the rites, but only one holds true to both the nature of the god Dionysus and the purging effects upon the Temple followers. It is the ritual of tragedy.

While known mostly as a god of wine and fertility, Dionysus is also intimately aligned with the development of the classic artform known as Greek tragedy. The earliest ritual celebrations honoring Dionysus involved the singing of epic poems by a chorus dressed as satyrs in goat skins (from which the term *tragoedia* is derived, meaning "goat song"). The chorus danced circularly and then counter-circularly around the Dionysian alter, concluding the ceremony in a cessation of all movement. These three divisions of the Dionysian ritual were named strophe ("movement"), antistrophe ("countermovement"), and epode ("afterpiece"). Later, spoken dialogue was added and, later still, dramatic action was incorporated into the celebration, each inspired by the original songs to Dionysus. Ultimately, the ceremony evolved into classic Greek tragedy, whose plays were performed during the festival to Dionysus upon a circular stage with the Dionysian alter at its center. As such, the tragic plays remained ritual celebrations to the god and personified what the ancient Greeks believed to be the essence of this god: his contrary yet somehow complementary attributes of tragedy and joy, of death and birth.

When the Dionysian ritual moved into the realm of tragic plays, it continued to reflect the circular, counter-circular and ceasing of movement central to the original goat-song ceremony. The plot carried a forward movement of action and expectation, followed by a dramatic reversal of fortune and great surprise in the audience, then concluding with a recognition of some truth previously hidden from the play's principal characters.

A Greek tragic play typically involved a worthy though flawed hero who is appointed a quest. During the pursuit of this quest, the hero invariably commits some small violation of divine expectation, such as failing to offer hospitality to a traveling stranger. The violation was usually described as resulting from hubris on the part of the hero. It would be a mistake, however, to equate hubris with obvious arrogance, as modern usage does. The original Greek use of the word was more akin to rushing forward. Impetuous might be the better equivalent to hubris, for the violation committed by the hero was often portrayed as involving nothing more than the quest itself. The hero is asserting his will in a vigorous effort to accomplish the quest, which becomes his downfall. Forward hubris unweights and turns the capricious winds of fate, reversing the hero's triumphant path. He is plunged into horrible suffering many times greater than the expected price of his minor offense. The audience is aghast.

Sophocles' *Oedipus the King* is regarded by many as the greatest of ancient Greek tragedy. The Kingdom of Thebes lies in squalor from a lengthy period of drought and disease and the king justly desires comfort for his subjects. He sends his brother-in-law, Creon, to the god Apollo to beg for relief. Creon returns with a message from the god: discover and exile the person who years ago killed the prior king, King Laius, and the kingdom will return to favor. Oedipus accepts this quest with a great force of purpose, genuinely wishing to cure the ills of his people. The audience is told that he is a good king with a noble character, and the audience embraces the king and his rightful cause. Oedipus interrogates many in the kingdom and learns that the prior king had been murdered by a nomad bandit at a crossroads. Oedipus next summons the blind prophet Tiresias for questioning, who answers only with pleas that this quest be abandoned. Frustrated, Oedipus accuses the prophet of being implicit in the murder, whereupon Tiresias succumbs to the questioning and declares that the murderer is both brother and father to his own children and both son and husband to his own mother. The audience thus learns that a law of the gods has been violated.

The fortunes of the king quickly reverse as he discovers though a series of disclosures and recollections that he is the adopted and not natural son of the parents who raised him, that he fled his original homeland to escape a prophesy that he would kill his father and marry his mother, that he quarreled with and killed a man at a crossroads and that he eventually traveled to Thebes where he won the hand of its widowed queen. It is Queen Jocasta who first realizes that she is the biological mother of Oedipus, recalling how she and King Laius had long ago abandoned and presumably killed their son to escape the same prophesy of murder and marriage. In desperate despair, Jocasta hangs herself. Oedipus enters the palace room where her body hangs dead and releases a cry of tortured agony. The truth that he is the murderer is suddenly revealed to him. He gently takes his queen's body down from the noose and removes long pins from a broach on her dress. King Oedipus plunges

the lengthy pins into his own eyes and blinds himself. As blood pours from the king's eyes, the chorus on stage laments the flawed nature of humanity and its powerlessness against the tides of destiny.

Needless to say, the suffering is so horrific, the violence so vehement and the result so disproportionate to the good, yet flawed, character of the king that the audience is deeply roused. Aristotle describes the effect as "cathartic." The audience members are purged of their mental, structural benchmarks. The rational, the sequential, the controllable are swamped. Overwhelmed by the power of mercurial fate and its spin upon the slightest unknowable turn, the audience is shocked into an awakening of sorts. That which seems is mere illusion. The assumed stability and sequence of ordinary life teeter along a spider's thread. Reality is instead buried secrets and upending floods. Rather than despairing, though, the effect is described by Aristotle as one of release, as though the mental constructs of an objective world are burdens from which one is freed. The weight of imprisoning structure is lifted and the world comes sensuously alive.

Friedrich Nietzsche in his first work, *The Birth of Tragedy*, contrasted this freeing spirit of Dionysus against Apollo's structured world of rationality. The spirit of Apollo, according to Nietzsche, can be witnessed in the epic poems of Homer, which exhibit a forward, linear course and hold to ethical rules and morals. The spirit of Dionysus, on the other hand, is witnessed in the works of great tragedy, which exhibit reversing and unmanageable courses that rupture the accepted status quo. And that which is generally accepted by humanity, Nietzsche later wrote, is of a fixed order opposed to true life. We rigidly impose our morals and truths and, in so doing, demean, exclude and manipulate. The *Oedipus* prophesy was realized because of the characters' blind attempts to avoid the prophesy. Misery is created by our blind attempts to thwart misery through the imposition of forward order. In Dionysus, though, we are gifted a realization of tragedy and our own part in its play, none of which can be thwarted. The controllable illusion of reality shatters. No longer surprised at each sudden tremor of fate, reality softens. No longer blinded by personal justification, we cease our frantic pursuits. Kindness becomes easy. In a reversing, unpredictable world, we need each other. Thriving connections and reliances appear. A *living* order emerges.

What secret rites were staged in the inner sanctum of the Dionysian Temple? An experience of the explosive turns of destiny? Of our own hidden hubris? Of our own tragic losses? And, within the dissolution of fluid tears, a new reality? A reconciliation of forward and reverse? Tragedy, perhaps, as a bringer of consciousness. Fracturing the objective mask we wear and revealing its artificial nature, so the mask is removed.

As they exited the Temple, the unmasked celebrants of Dionysus exhibited such an exuberance of spirit and carnival of absurd that they appeared mad. But were they mad? Was their state a temporary trance celebrating the uninhibited and inebriated? Most scholars claim yes, that Dionysus represents the innate wildness of human nature. Their behavior was chaotic, succumbing to the seductiveness of disorder and taboo. Yet the nature of tragedy provides clues otherwise. If one can accept that the effect of the Dionysian ritual mirrored in some fashion its pattern, then the celebrants were not mere anarchists. Their madness was not purely the absence of rational. It is possible that the initiates of Dionysus were stunned into a vision of sorts, a new paradigm risen from the emptied old. Their antics celebrate not a lack of order but a rising new dynamic order.

As the life of Oedipus and its pattern reveal, not just linear movement and radical reversal, but in the end an *epode*: the sudden, powerful revelation of a mystery deep and hidden.

Alchemy

MYSTERIES AND MISUNDERSTANDINGS DEFINE ALCHEMY, that ancient trade of chemists and madmen. During an uninterrupted period of four centuries, seekers pursued the Great Work of creating the Philosopher's Stone through strange, esoteric formulas of transmutation. The quest was one of the many pursuits of the incomparable Isaac Newton, whose studies in this craft contributed to his breakthroughs in other fields. Robert Boyle, generally credited as the founder of modern chemistry, honed his rigorous scientific method as an alchemist. The pursuit of the Great Work has elicited numerous contributions to the human endeavor, but what exactly is the Philosopher's Stone?

To understand, one must first comprehend the two foundational tenets of alchemy: 1) that the small is mirrored in the great, the microcosm in the macrocosm, and vice versa (captured in alchemy's maxim "as above, so below; as below, so above"), and 2) that both such spheres are comprised of two elements—substance (the coarse, or fixed) and essence (the subtle, or fluid).

Alchemists believed that, through the legendary alchemical process, base metals could be transmuted into noble metals (notably, lead into gold, but other chemical transmutations were attempted). More importantly, they believed that such a physical transmutation would be mirrored in higher spheres, thus honoring the maxim "as below, so above." The individual will acquire a higher state of being, including longevity of life, godly wisdom or other divine attributes. This belief in mirrored transmutation was not only a quest for the individual person, though. A transformation of earthly matter could effect a transformation of all of heaven and earth, a new creation of both above and below, a creation known as the Philosopher's Stone. Such was the power and allure of this ageless pursuit.

The quest for the Philosopher's Stone across Egypt, India, the Middle East and Europe led to vastly disparate and obscure paths. Alchemy became associated with secret, cryptic arts. There was also no agreement on the base material to be worked and transformed. For some, the material was not a metal but was the human person, and alchemy branched into the quasi-religious cult of Hermeticism. For all the confusing variants of alchemy, two primary sources were generally honored: the ancient text known as the Emerald Tablet and the ancient sigil defining the alchemical movement known as the Ouroboros, the symbol of a coiled snake consuming its own tail.

The Emerald Tablet is believed to have been written in the second century CE by Hermes Trismegistus (Thrice Great Hermes), who is generally attributed as the father of alchemy. The author's otherworldly name hints at the otherworldliness attributed to his text. The legendary Tablet is said to hold the secret formula to accomplish the Magnum Opus, the creation of the Philosopher's Stone. Countless historical interpretations of the Tablet's formulation exist but, regardless of the interpretation, its mystical status as the founding text of alchemy endures:

> 'Tis certain, most true,
> above as below, below as above.

*The one begot both essence and substance and is the
child of the two.*
The sun its father, the moon its mother.
*The wind carried it within and bore it from its womb;
the earth its nursemaid.*
*It is power and perfection here and now, but is
perfected when weaved into existence.*
*Through humility, gentleness and wisdom, separate the
volatile from the fixed.*
*The subtle shall adhere and ascend, where above and
below join in union.*
*Descending, its power will overwhelm all things,
both breath and flesh.*
Each part shall equal the whole.
*From this process sight will be given and the earth
transformed in the manner it was first formed.*
*Thus speaks Hermes Trismegistus, father of the tri-part
alchemy of everything.*
Thus spoken, it is complete, lacking in nothing.

The quest to achieve the Philosopher's Stone has historically involved a deciphering of the mysterious formula outlined in the Emerald Tablet. Following introductory recitations of the power and history of the Stone, the Tablet instructs the alchemist to separate with "humility, gentleness and wisdom" the fixed from the volatile. Thus the initial stage involves a breaking down of stability. The walls of the base element are somehow weakened in order to separate its earthy components from its airy. The material must become unfixed, freed of its hardened boundaries. In pursuing this stage, early alchemists perfected methods of distillation that physically separate subtle matter (that which evaporates) from coarse matter (that which settles).

Next it is intoned that, once separated, the subtle shall adhere and ascend. Adhere to what? The Tablet does not say, but unquestionably relationship arises from the separation. From an alchemical standpoint, this adherence was often viewed as the first of many joinings of opposites. The moist, receptive agent released from the distillation perhaps adheres to a dry, active agent (receptive mercury or quicksilver, for example, with sulfur). Oppositions are coupled. However, the Tablet states that the subtle agents shall themselves adhere, shall connect to each other and ascend. How to reconcile these contrary concepts?

Here is where alchemy's other founding authority, the Ouroboros, may assist. This symbol of a snake or dragon consuming its own tail is etched prominently within alchemical texts, but what is its connection to alchemy? As a first impression, the Ouroboros appears to question the entire concept of one's self. It depicts the snake as inherently possessing a type of reciprocity. It is both prey, being fed to another in sacrifice, and is predator, feeding upon that prey. The irreconcilable opposition of predator and prey is presented as a single reality. Like day sacrificed to night so to be nourished and reborn as new day. Or summer into winter where summer is not extinguished. Summer is not negated by winter, but reclines and rests in its arms. They exist as one reality. One aspect is material and active but soon exhausted; its other aspect is unfixed and mysterious but rejuvenating. Not two realities. Not conflict, but mutuality. Reciprocal risings and fallings. Nourishing and nourished. Like the ever-mixing dark-light from dawn to dusk back to dawn, death and birth are linked in reciprocal dependence as a single self.

Perhaps, in the dissolution of their hard margins, the newly subtle matter *realizes* an adherence, a connection with its twinned self. Winter is no longer viewed by summer as a frightening negation but as an intimate embrace. One feeding the other. Coupling rather than opposing. Inside rests in outside, the positive charge in the negative. The dry sun scatters and refreshes in the moist rain. The bounded self reclines and is reborn within its unbounded self. Oppositions ever-present and adjusting, ever moving between. One.

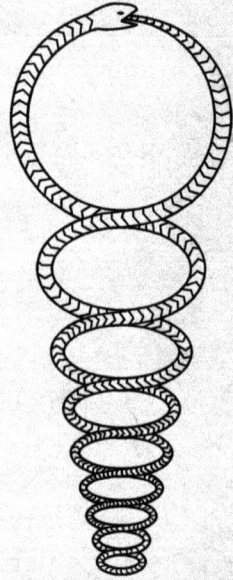

Following the distillation of the base element and the commencement of adherence, while again not clear in the text of the Emerald Tablet, alchemists hold that the process enters a lengthy period of gestation. The Great Work moves into its night stage, as it is called. Alchemists claim that a thick mist descends, clouding any observation of the agents during this period. A time of wait and hope must be endured. The alchemist knows not if the Work has been properly sparked and awaits a clearing of the mist in its own time and manner. The agents exist in a space between what was and what might be. All lies shrouded in uncertainty.

The Tablet describes this mysterious time as one of ascension. It states that, having adhered, the subtle-realmed agents begin to ascend. Again, the Ouroboros may provide hints at interpretation of this stage. The coiled snake is not coupled in circularity alone. The single reality is not merely revolving, not endlessly repeating itself. It is also transmuting. The snake is springing into *new* life. Not simply re-formed, but rising differently, re-energized, unique. The hardened, dull lead awakens as malleable, lustrous gold.

We consider the possibility that, during the gestation period, the distilled subtle agents do not tamely adhere and ascend.

Instead, they realize an adherence as they awaken as a larger self. A rebirth is occurring at each stage, creating each new level. The adherence *is* the ascension. The joining of contradiction accomplishes a wider identity and, thus, an ascension. Each agent is born again into a larger self, and again and again into larger selves, ascending in size unto the pinnacle.

We are not made aware of reality; reality is made self-aware in us. That which resides outside of us (and where we too reside) is the focus; not our own awareness or experiences. What does reality long to experience? Can we offer it our own? What does reality long to express? Can we offer it ourselves? Who are we together?

Ultimately, at some unknowable and critical moment, a chasm is leaped, a threshold broken. An overwhelming connection is sparked. The Tablet gives no more description than "above and below join in union." This union is stated almost matter-of-factly, but make no mistake: this is the moment, the Great Opus, the Philosopher's Stone. A reciprocal coupling of earth (the manifest, the knowable) with heaven (the mysterious, the uncreated). A surrender and consummation, a marriage, a joining of above and below, of divine and mortal. Yet this union fires neither precious gold nor heavenly paradise. It is a consummation of both, of lead and gold, of heaven and earth. The moment is wondrous and wild, a completion of each in the other.

This culmination of the Work is not the conclusion of the Work, however. Lastly, the Tablet tells us that "descending, its power will overwhelm all things." A force, or power, or animate living essence is released from the joining. "Each part shall equal the whole. ...sight will be given and the earth transformed..."

A great genesis rebirths the universe. As below in the humble, so above in the vast.

A Cradling of Contradiction

That which is shy and wondrous stirs within the confusion, longing for expression. Conflicts surround, although we sense timeless promises groping toward completion in this place. Here is where we belong, outside clarity, where dawning mysteries whisper of approach.

Einstein theorized over a century ago that reality contains no solid unmoving platform from which time or space can be objectively measured. Everything in the universe moves, so space and time exist as a relationship between relative motions. They are not objective things but an operation between things. Einstein further asserted that time and space share their own relationship. They are not independent even of each other. An inseverable bond holds them as one, as spacetime.

As Mandelbrot discovered in his study of fractals, the physical world too is layered in intimate relationships. Like space and time determining each other, the patterns within the tiniest scale replicate themselves into the largest and into every layer between. Though not precisely replicated; instead, the patterns allow individual freedom. A connection of mirroring and deviating.

Similarly, in nonlinear systems such as weather and bird flocks, the action of the tiniest participant spreads through widening levels into the whole—a type of real-time fractal. Each participant acts independently yet is constantly aligning, dependent. This same movement dynamically pools bees into widening scales of decision-making. Individuals freed from regulation naturally move within exponentially adjusting attractions. Independence and dependence in relationship, interlacing in dynamic orderings.

Nature moves in unceasing mutuality. Summer dissolves to rest within winter, as day splinters to renew within night. Ants and birds wander afar to discover and return, gifting new sources of life. Are these movements in conflict? Is winter outside of summer? Are wandering birds outside the flock? Is death outside of life? Or are they interwoven? Surrendering to each other in turn, inseparable. Like heat and cold, heat thrives only by reason of its lack. Together they are the twinned movements of winds and waters and life!

Within these graces, the value of death may be received, but not death as a thing. Alone it is separation and heartache. Its value rises only in its relationship with life. Together life! The way of life. Things are no longer things. Opposites give way and entwine as a single movement.

Perhaps, too, the value of pain may be received, yet not as an alone thing. Alone it is the distress of conflict, dysfunction, loss. The value of pain rises only in its relationship with love. Together love! The way of love. Pain interwoven with sharings and joy. Each submitting. Inseparable.

A hidden treasure stirs toward awakening. The soul longs to somehow embrace the tension of things. The sharings between hurting and healing, brokenness and belonging. A yearning to reconcile with all we can no longer point a finger at. A cradling of contradiction, where contrary divisions touch and exchange as one movement. A fluidness to sorrow and joy, distress and comfort, presence and absence. The clash of conflict resolves, embraces in its unbroken play, in its vital livingness.

The striving soul comes to rest in the wide sway of all it cradles.

Shamanism

"'Sublimity,' Hauptmann says, panting, 'you know what that is, Pfennig?' He is tipsy, animated, almost prattling. Never has Werner seen him like this. 'It's the instant when one thing is about to become something else.'"

—ANTHONY DOERR, *ALL THE LIGHT WE CANNOT SEE*

ANTHROPOLOGISTS HAVE LONG WONDERED how the shamans of indigenous people could have learned the complex botanical chemistry of the healing plants they use. In the rainforest, for example, the tribal shaman chooses from among nearly one million species of plant to concoct intricate pharmaceuticals through the use of but a handful. It is assumed that this knowledge was passed down through generations of trial and error learning. Yet, if you ask the shamans, they offer a different explanation. As outlined in anthropologist Jeremy Narby's *The Cosmic Serpent*, the indigenous shamans claim that it is the plants themselves who teach them their art. The essential nature of a shaman, Narby concludes from his studies, is a receptivity to a world that unfolds itself and instructs those who enter. A pliable world bending to open hearts and eyes, longing to share mysteries poetic and beautiful.

The process for entry into these lands of the shaman often involves the use of hallucinogens but certainly not universally. Other paths include fasting, sleeplessness, drum rhythms, dancing and rituals loosening the structure of rigid identities.

In the initial stages, the shaman experiences a period of intense anxiety. A sickening in the stomach foreshadows the opening of personal perceptions. An experience of the soul striving toward a "becoming."

Next, the shaman's sense of self is humbled. They describe a growing awareness of the powerful vastness which surrounds and, amid such forces, of the littleness of self. Not in a frightening manner, however. The experience is instead one of childlike wonder in the face of such overwhelming vulnerability. The assumptions of reality move from individual self and self-will to a humbling reverence for some vital immensity. The hard lines defining the individual break down within this great vitality beyond the self. Sustained or destroyed we move in each moment. We are given gifts, and as gifts we are given. Rather than paralyzed in these forces, though, the shaman describes the experience as moving toward livingness and lightness. Crossing a threshold beyond words or thought, the shaman is invited into a secret world.

This voyage of the shaman into otherworldly lands has also been described in terms of the *axis mundi*, or axis of the world. Across numerous indigenous cultures, a common tradition tells of a twisted vine or braided rope that reaches upward from the earth into the heavens. Guarded by a twinned serpent or dragon, the shaman learns the secrets of passage past this barrier to a place where life-giving knowledge is gained and returned to the people. The mystical power gifted has been paradoxically described as both destroyer and creator, the shaman's power both undermining order and creating order out of chaos. (Narby, pps. 15-17 [Tarcher/Putnam paperback ed. 1999])

In this otherworldly land, rainforest shamans tell of subtle beings who emerge from rivers, lakes, foliage and even soil. Named *maninkari*, or "hidden ones," these spirit beings are also called *ashaninka*, or "our fellows," meaning ancestors. There is a closeness, a sense of intimacy with these creatures and their world. The beings communicate with the shaman in a language of signs where one must be attentive to similarities among patterns presented. A connection between patterns occurs to the shaman, signaling a coupled relationship. For example, the antidote to a certain snake venom is revealed in an image of the snake's fangs, which the shaman connects to a plant containing similarly shaped hooks—a sign that the two are complements: poison and cure. Seeing correspondences is essential to the shamans' learning. Reality becomes twinned and twisting, much like the two-headed guardian and twisted rope accessing this world. This language reflects the mirrored, refractory nature of the reality entered. A male/female principle (also imaged as any number of other polarities such as light and dark) dominates the landscape—binary oppositions that are reconciled and thus received as wisdom. The shamans describe this method of communication as *tsai yoshtoyoshto*, literally "language twisting-twisting." As one shaman explains: "…twisted language brings me close but not too close—with normal words I would crash into things—with twisted ones I circle around them—I can see them clearly." (Narby, pps. 98-99)

Narby discusses at length the correlations between the twinned and twisting healing power of the shamans and the life-creating power of DNA and its twinned spirals. He theorizes that the otherworldly encounters experienced by the shamans may involve consciousness on a molecular level, permitting exchanges with the living DNA of the lush rainforest. Knowledge is conveyed, according to Narby, not through trial and error but from its source—the twisted ladder DNA source of life. Or perhaps, from the source of the source, that power or sacred essence providing a reverse complementary shape to the universe. The twinned and spiraled creative source of all things.

It is time. Our own soul strives toward becoming. Without the need of aids, we move our attention outward into the world, trusting it to reveal itself in its own way and time. A world who allows us entry and instructs us through reciprocal patterns. Its vastness surrounds and deepens. We surrender, childlike, vulnerable. We cannot own, cannot know, cannot plan, cannot control. The beginnings of something else. Something living and lovely. A growing awareness of a twinned world, relational. No longer of contradiction but of attraction. Of ancient indivisible bonds. A twisting world, like a song, beautiful, where we dance in its music, where we belong. Tears fall in loveliness. In such trembling simplicity of love.

This book has hesitated before now to use the word love, but what else could it mean? Has that not been the dream all along? A fierce undying hope in healing through connection. Healing not of the individual but of relationship, of family, of community. Healing between.

A surrendering love healing all of creation, as the first sparks attract and thread and billow into fire.

Loop Quantum Gravity

PHYSICIST CARLO ROVELLI, in his marvelously understated book *Reality Is Not What It Seems*, presents in non-scientific terms the latest thinking in theoretical physics. One of the early collaborators developing the theory of loop quantum gravity, Rovelli turns his creative touch to mainstream writing to paint a rich and delicate portrait of reality. The work is more than a descriptive account, however. The author attempts to capture what he believes to be the essence of science: an unending questioning of established knowledge. For science, according to Rovelli, is the antithesis of doctrine. It is an expression of the quest of every human heart, born of curiosity and ever-drawn toward discovery.

While our book here is incapable of approaching the complex subjects Rovelli unravels, it nonetheless attempts to express certain shimmerings which float to the surface. Foremost is the long-unanswered puzzle in theoretical physics of how to reconcile relativity theory with quantum theory. Einstein's general relativity theory, which operates in the realm of larger matter, explains its universe in terms of continuous curved spacetime and gravity. Quantum theory, which operates in the realm of the subatomic, explains its universe in terms of indeterminant, discontinuous events and relations among discrete quanta (individual packets). Each describes a world utterly inconsistent with the other with no (yet) apparent connection between the two. Rovelli brings to this question the theory of loop quantum gravity (admitting that the theory competes with an alternative one, string theory, for recognition). Under the quantum gravity viewpoint, space consists of small packets of gravity that interact with one another. Like the packaged energy of atoms comprising matter and the quantum packets of photons comprising electromagnetic waves, Rovelli believes that tiny quanta of gravity comprise space itself. They do not exist in space, as do atoms and photons, but interplay with each other to create the fabric that is space. Space is not a container that holds the universe but is itself a living web of interactions.

The relationship between the two realms of relativity and quantum, according to Rovelli, is a matter of scale. He compares the relationship to that existing between photons and electromagnetic waves. Electromagnetic waves are the big picture while discrete photons are the elemental components. Discontinuous interactions between the individual photons form the waves' consistency and continuity. In this same manner, space (or, as discussed below, spacetime) is the big picture, while quantum grains of gravity are the elemental components. Teeming looping interactions between packets of gravity create the consistency and continuity of space. Quantum laws operate on the elemental discontinuous scale while relativity laws operate on the large continuous scale.

What shimmers here is not the theory itself, regardless of its novelty and possibilities for understanding reality; rather, its implications. Despite the surface of things which exhibit a uniformity of appearance, everything, even space itself, is in essence a turbulent interaction. Is purely relational. Equally amazing is how the relationships between gravity quanta build loops, which themselves interconnect and interact. At the infinitesimal level of reality known as the Planck scale, space foams like the sea, churning in interconnectivity and looping in collaborative connections. In the same manner that convection currents and ant colonies spring from individual interactivity, our continuous, large-scale world springs from an individual, relational sub-world. Two twinned worlds, each ever-present and dependent.

A final shimmering from this picture of reality is that its implications are not limited to space alone. The same inter-activity comprising the web of space creates time. As space is composed of individual quanta in living exchanges, time is composed of individual variables in mutual exchange. Discrete events occur in different rates of change, and time rises from the variance between them. Like space no longer being viewed as an objective container for reality, time is no longer viewed as an objective forward flow of reality. It is not a measure of change but a relationship of changes. For example, the time interval of a heartbeat arises only in relation to a different time interval, such as that of a swinging pendulum. The continuity of large-scale time leaps from teeming exchanges between disparate rates of change. Twinned time.

All of reality—*everything*—arises from a mutuality between continuous and discontinuous worlds. The large and uniform miraculously spring from the small and indeterminate. Reality is the reciprocal turnings, the collaborations between.

Anxiety

THE INTENT HERE is to neither trivialize nor validate anxiety, an often-crippling disease so widely suffered. The disease is particularly cruel for youth, who are becoming afflicted at exponentially exploding rates. Current statistics claim 25% of children aged 13 to 18 suffer from an anxiety disorder. Yet parents sleeplessly fret at a threat far exceeding any statistic. Anxiety is overcoming the generation that is our children.

The disease arrives with the slightest half-breath that cannot be completed. A whisper of flutterings dance in the stomach, hardly noticeable but to the sufferer. To the sufferer, this tiny whisper echoes of the flood that may follow. The fluttering sensations lengthen and grow into waves that rise upward through the body and into the mind. The sufferer assures himself or herself that all is good; that there is nothing to fear. But the body claims otherwise. Frighteningly, a tide of apprehension overtakes and overflows.

The prevalence of this disease cannot be wholly dismissed as a disorder. It carries within the suffering a sensitive intuition that we disregard at our peril. A radio signal of sorts from beyond accepted reality. A "canary in the coal mine" who is the first to signal impending danger. Something is amiss in our world.

An anxiety sufferer need only pause to realize the origins of the overwhelming stress. Among the defective structures is the unrelenting tick-tock-tick-tock of objective time. While time claims to move in a precise segmented fashion, it crowds ever-more demands into each segment. The experience is one of desperate franticness. Also, linear time ties events into an endless chain of sequences. The slightest misstep in the present moment can have disastrous consequences to one's whole life. Anxiety pleads to the sufferer: "It is too much! This day and its constant pressure. This life and its daunting future." The sufferer *dreads* tomorrows and the unrelenting tick-tock of the clock.

Another such objective ruler over our lives is money or, for our youth, academic grades. We calculate and count as our bellies churn in fear of disaster. One's welfare is evaluated alone and vulnerable. A world of winning or losing.

So many false promises: the "freedom" of cars and instead the indignities and tragedies of the highway; or the "connections" of computers and smartphones and instead the addictive programming and descent into isolation and loneliness. Most often, it is not one stressor triggering anxiety but a complex collection of them. Conceptual systems bombarding the nervous system, rendering each of us alone and exposed.

Mentally conceived systems do not stop with the external world either. Our painful social anxiety points to another prominent stressor: our perception of self. As with the rest of the objective world, we view ourselves in conceptual terms, as a defined thing. Yet at some unspoken level we realize the falseness to this image which must be unerringly projected and defended. Social situations heighten our sense of pretension. The entire masquerade rises to the surface. A rising wave of anxiety signaling the presence of an error in the program.

The program. Perhaps all of these stressors possess a single source: the hidden method of human perception. The objective thought-mood system is itself the painful stressor, not the causes it blames. Anxiety is a natural response to being trapped, as if locked in airless box. Rather than physically confined, however, we realize a different type of imprisonment. Enclosed in thoughts, moods and emotions and their ceaseless demands, we feel trapped within our own mental shell. Each day is dominated by inner dictates, and the person is diminished as a person. We are denied the freedom to contribute our uniqueness to the world.

Anxiety marks a turning point. Robbed of an outlet for our personhood, we can no longer conform. Can no longer behave well, tamely following a defective approach to reality. For how the mind speaks to us is obsolete, its demands hierarchical, violent, demeaning. Flawed. Our world is not fixed, not available to structured thought-moods. Not stuck in right or wrong, winning or losing, favored or rejected. We are opened to the possibility of something new. Anxiety provides us an excuse, a freedom to deviate.

"Anxiety is the great birth-giver," as Jean Gebser writes. The experience of an awakening soul.

The wonder of creation is rising, pleading for us to notice, to move our focus away from the incessant push of life-draining mentality. Everything is unsettled, in every facet of life, so we leave it unsettled. We mistrust our frantic craving for calm and look elsewhere for our peace. To a power flooding into the world, breaching the pretend. Not power as our mind has defined it. Different. Illogical peace. Our anxiety irrationally close to an intimacy. To a dignity, drawing our attention outward. We notice small moments and simple things. The sounds of children playing, the feel of raindrops on the skin, or the taste of morning air. We observe decentralized movements of humble livingness, and they in turn awaken within our attention. Not awareness vaguely in-the-moment, but lit upon something magical, something magically shared, received and given. A collaboration. Birds, insects, clouds, trees, people—how they come alive within our notice. A genuineness is sensed in the interchange. A healing. The hard lines of division soften. We possess and are possessed, as though sharing a vital breath.

Despite all unsettlings, we awaken outside of ourselves. A reciprocal reality free of cause and consequence, for only the relation matters. The immediate exchange. The depth of community it intimates. Something attracting us, involving us, seeking our interplay with it. Our genuine world opens to us, as does our genuine selves.

We feel it. It is here. Stirring within us and echoing in this world. Giving rise to a gift so simple: a turn of priorities. Our relationships become everything. Our shared exchanges essential. More important than any aspect of the severed self and its emotions. More important than any thought-truth. Our outer world opens in dignity, in connections humble and reliant. So precious, regardless of whether challenging or pleasing. Irreplaceable. Such *primacy* of tending to them. Of living within them.

Existence remains difficult, yet deeply comforting, for we now know what is essential. We finally see where it lives. We have found the genuine.

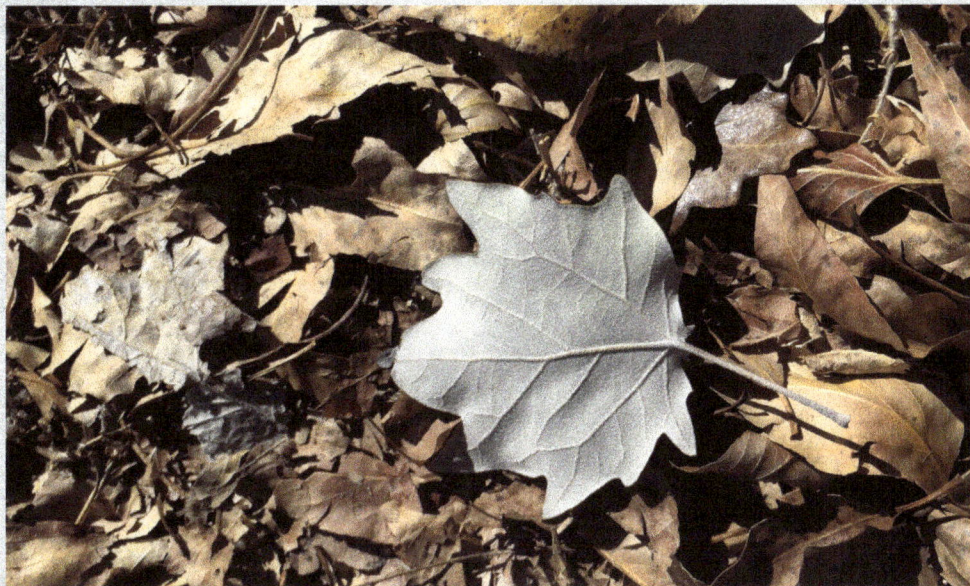

The End

The end of a lengthy journey requires a lengthy journey. How long has it been? Surely years. Decades. A lifetime since the first quaking of reality. A lifetime of weakening of walls. Loss, heartbreak, anxiety—all the tears of living. So many joys as well—family, friends, laughter and sharing. Sharing…strange how even the tears, when shared, become part of the joy. Part of something beyond itself.

There is no way this is going to say what it longs to say. For what it longs to say is that saying accomplishes nothing, means nothing. It's more and still more of the same nothing. The same aloneness—the separation from and talking at you without exchange. The same stifling knowledge without interaction. The same isolation without sharing. Everything and everyone like pillars of salt, untouching.

Beware. So fine the line between self-loss and self-godhood. Both involve a recognition of falseness in old truths. Both leave deceptive structures behind. Yet the second claims to see clearly a great newness, asserts some shattering insight or wisdom or holiness. Here lies the last self-deception. Here the last remnant of the old world hides. The last vestiges of linear and logical. To uphold <u>anything</u> is hubris. To presume we have the answer is more of the same folly. Any claim of knowledge reinforces the revolving wheel of contrary claims. More ruins from this departing world. Our awakening is not a gain but a fall, a purging!

The long journey weakens the walls until, at some unknowable moment, exhaustion overwhelms. Exhausted of solving. Exhausted of all that must be upheld. The broken pieces that can no longer be desperately pulled together. Exhausted of time. The push and forward. What does it mean to reach a destination? What is forward? Is anything there? None of this involves any sense of enlightenment. Not a gain where we acquire clarity. It is always a loss. A loss of stability and, as such, of vision. A challenge to who we are and what this world is. No longer is there a possibility of choosing. We cannot plan and do, cannot solve. Nothing more can be done; it is over.

The ultimate challenge of the quest is inevitably the quest itself. We finally face the end. The end of everything. No dream fulfilled. No other side. No resolution of the conflict and pain. Our suffering continues unabated. No one is healed. Our long journey has served no purpose. We have participated in no new world, no coming. Not as in some romance movie before the happy ending. Real. The world is not healed; it is raging, unhealed! Our work is over; nothing has changed. Messes spill everywhere and we cannot fight another minute. Cannot journey another step. Cannot hope another dream. Nothing will ever change. Really. We face this truth. We cry. Round full tears of failure, of a finality without comfort.

What is left when no one is healed and nothing has changed? When no more can be done?

We don't know. The only certainty is that conflict will not be resolved, is unresolvable. Yet we cannot be left alone in this terrible truth. Something must remain for us. …A single word is offered, but it is merely a word, set in defined boundaries and fraught with hidden assumptions. It is not an answer, but it is…something, something to consider when at the end:

Forgive.

A mere word, but not a word when coming alive. When experienced, it grows. Ignites something. Redefines perception.

At the end when nothing is mended, when crises can be lived not a moment longer, we become consumed in overwhelming anger or surrendered in overwhelming forgiveness. Surrendered to everything. Forgiving to everyone. To the pain, the maddening dysfunction. We forgive the bitter end. Forgive the lack of resolution. Forgive conflict. Forgive ourselves. Forgive loss. Forgive each upset and upheaval. Without expectation, without needing the forgiveness accepted. Forgive as only one at the end could possibly forgive. Without any sense of justification. Without any purpose to be achieved. There is <u>nothing</u> left but to forgive. Difficult, personal, in front of us, unresolved. No justice. No righting of wrongs or healing of pain. We do not even forgive as much as allow forgiveness, for it floods upon us when we can do no more. A flowing mercy, with nothing beyond.

Which is, though, of itself, other things. When forgiveness enters without wanting change or acceptance, an opening appears. Creation in the tiniest of corners. The wall surrounding self unlocks. We emerge into a world no longer excluded from us. No longer judgeable. No longer chained to expectation. We no longer regard the world as logical or with logic. Nothing understandable. Everything so forgivable, so deserving of mercy, despite the failings.

Something lets go. Some grip releases.

An essence from beyond the stars rushes in. Innocence and compassion touch us. Profoundly touch us. More than forgiven, we are baptized in the tempest. Anointed into a land of painlove, of lovepain, of abandoning abiding love.

So difficult to describe. Not an end of conflict or suffering. Distinctions and differences clash everywhere. We simply forgive, without needing change. For nothing does change and, therein, everything changes.

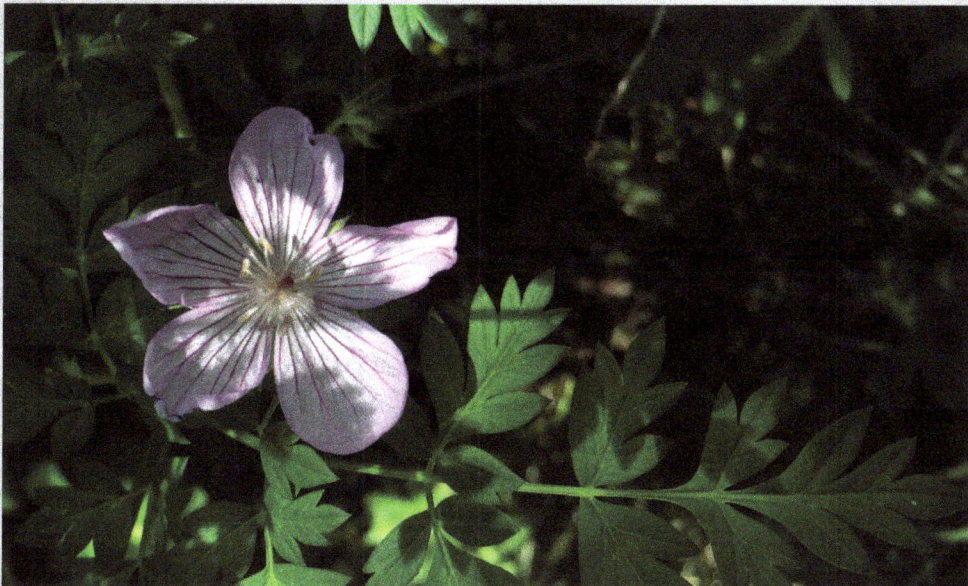

The Gift

IN ENTERING THE END, in allowing loss and mercy, we awaken to a wondrous gift.

This book does not pretend to know what is bestowed. How to imagine the unimaginable? No matter how or when it comes, it never comes as expected. No matter how well prepared. No matter how long awaited.

From our long travels, though, inspirations have carried hints. If the patterns are genuine, we are released. The shell of objective seeing and knowing breaks. Conflict becomes turbulence, like precious winds and waters welcoming us home— nondirectional, decentralized, relational *goodness*. Cause and assertion become attraction and belonging. Living exchanges and rhythms surround. Sharing lives in every direction. A world ever-rearranging, adjusting, rare, while ever-reliant, nested, safe. Where the small and humble shape the large and grand. Where, like birds, we are freed and bound together. Where, like trees, we shelter and are sheltered from. A giving which receives.

While before emotions flared at each malfunction of logical order, emotions turn to reverence, to overwhelming gratefulness. Such childlike awe at this world's workings, at its wild carefulness. Mysteries into which we become ourselves. Humbling our heart, to share in such wonder.

The defined earth is shattered. Conceptual reality loses meaning. The linear and logical, our fixed judgments, cease their dominance. The unimaginable has come. Is here.

a time of difficult reorientation,
of incorporating the gifts bestowed,
of reconciling separate worlds

…this rough magic
I here abjure; …
    …I'll break my staff,
Bury it certain fathoms in the earth,
And, deeper than did ever plummet sound,
I'll drown my book.

    …O, rejoice
Beyond a common joy, and set it down
With gold on lasting pillars. In one voyage
Did Claribel her husband find at Tunis;
And Ferdinand, her brother, found a wife
Where he himself was lost; Prospero, his dukedom
In a poor isle; and all of us, ourselves
When no man was his own.

—WILLIAM SHAKESPEARE, *THE TEMPEST*

The Return

A Knitting Together

Returning with a Token

Our homeland calls to us, and we heed its familiar voice. As with the many challenges already faced, however, re-entry is difficult. There is an initial impulse of rejection. A sense of frustration at the pettiness of opinion and conflict. Yet we are not above the common world. It is our home, the land in which our families dwell, where our ancestors toiled, where our hearts reside. So we return to daily life.

The return presents another critical crossroads. In re-entering forward time, we can easily be re-engulfed in its demands. Deadlines, worries and expectations overwhelm our attention. Entertainments plead for our escape into them. All that has been experienced at such a cost may be so easily lost into memory as somehow unreal. As though they never happened. The demands directly in front of us are real, not vague notions of depths rising and worlds joining. The memory of the gift will fade and die.

Immediately upon the return, each must remain open to receiving a unique icon from the far realm. If attentive, the experience bestowed in the recesses of reality will materialize in the form of a token or sanctuary. Perhaps a stone, or jewel or serpentine stick appears on the path and attracts itself to you. Or you pause at a bend in the trail, or in your room or upon some familiar place awakening to you. Mysteriously holding for you the energies of the deep. Your caduceus. This token is critical to the return, although not as a reminder of the vital depths. The token is not a memorial; it carries no meaning of what the depths represent. On the contrary, the icon suspends assertion, provides space around our intentions. Returns us to where we are, to the unmediated journey. Noticing the small; unafraid of confusion; watchful for discovery. A living encounter reappearing again and again...

... the turbulences rising around us may be, not painful storms we must navigate, but the entry of something extraordinary, the coming of Venus, of rarity and love.

the beautiful natural wilderness of loss of certainty, of loss of understanding, its contours rolling and unpredictable. the rustling breath of life. finally, not to be feared but celebrated, like the magical angle of dark-light at dawn or dusk, the great uncertainty lives, and is lived.

our world shattered and scattered as if dust in whirling storms, yet from deep within the painful disorder a mysterious silence rises, a glimmer of possibility. something other than empty concepts and counter-concepts. something beyond the law of this land. oddly, a great hope.

the deceit everywhere at play, unperceived as deceit even by those who plot it. the self-deception at the heart of human nature and how our own treachery cannot be far removed. we mistrust our own intentions, realize the blindness of our objective perceptions. a deviation in thought.

what is the boundary of a pattern which is stable yet which unceasingly interchanges itself with its surroundings? something comes alive, becomes an involvement between the self and the world. something that cannot be measured. its margins unfixed. self spreads and absorbs outside of self. outside ourselves are we born.

we begin to see through the uncaring, hardened thought-order around us into the natural, beautiful ordering that is life. tears may fall in the realization of so much goodness; deep satisfying goodness. meaning is not a thing that can be named or explained *but is our part in the living goodness. a place where we enter and contribute in a widening, vibrant eternity.*

as if astray in a magical forest, we allow each to rise and disappear without judgment, without a required role to play. an honoring of other over identity, as the old order of answer-making has lost relevance. and behold: that something which must be honored above all else, that beauty or innocence or nameless goldenness appears, which forever beckons us home.

autumn winds through trees. nothing rational. no sequential order. no wisdom practical or useful. yet as the most secret branches are reached, a strange freeing kind of madness moves. full of failings, of endings, of admissions and forgivings; full of the moment, a ragged windswept redemption from which the vibrant depths stir.

in aporia, in that state without markings of place or direction, one is guided toward a land where goodness lives, and pervades, and soaks deep.

like walking sideways across round fields, what can be said of direction? none exists, whether in time or motion, and so it all pools, and bonds soak in. an achingly beautiful shared livingness that lives beyond its seeable forms. where we become a part of something beyond us that nonetheless defines us. defines us in a new way. a loss of the separated self, in which the genuine self is found.

the ritual of ashes. it breaks the chains. it frees those bound.

we are gifted a realization of tragedy, of a reversing, unpredictable world. the weight of objective structure falls and all comes sensuously alive. in vulnerability, kindness becomes easy. we need each other. thriving connections and reliances appear. a living order emerges.

the possibility that humanity is awakening to nature's decentralized movements and emergent method of change. a movement-change-time pattern that swarms, attracts, doubles and creates.

a mystical power paradoxically described as both destroyer and creator, both undermining order and creating order out of chaos. a twisting world, like a song, beautiful, where we dance in its music, where we belong. tears fall in loveliness. in such trembling simplicity of love.

twilight time, resonating, local. a leaf opening to the moist dew. needing and receiving, providing through its undying exchange.

the soul's longing to cradle the tension of things, the sharings between hurting and healing, brokenness and belonging. Disorder and order in unceasing exchange.

at the end, the deep difficulties soften in invitation. they ask for surrender to the pain. a sense of profound compassion permeates. a dignity which our logical words have so long denied. the grace of innocence everywhere.

an essence from beyond the stars rushes in. more than forgiven, we are baptized in the tempest. anointed into a land of painlove, of lovepain, of abandoning abiding love…

Upon our return, a palladium falls to earth as from heaven— an icon assuring us that the overwhelming embrace shared within the depths was real, and preserving its intimacy within the wakefulness of return. Not a fanciful dream which scatters upon waking, but a powerful union which endures and heals.

Pharmakon

THE EXPERIENCE OF A NEW REALITY is not the living of it.

Jacque Derrida, the renown French philosopher, probed the workings of human language and described what he believed to be its blind spot. Words do not possess intrinsic meaning but find meaning only through reference to a contrast. Every concept is understood in the context of its opposition, typically as part of a presence-absence dichotomy, such as true/false or light/dark. His famous study involved a reading of Plato's *Phaedrus* and its use of the word "pharmakon." Depending on the context of its use, pharmakon is employed by Plato to refer either to healing or to sickness. Derrida notes how language demands a choice between the contradictory meanings. While reading the text, we unthinkingly assign the correct definition to the word within the context it is used. However, it goes completely unnoticed (blind spot) that a single word holds both senses. The mind cannot grasp that the word's meaning may involve contrary meanings.

Derrida's analysis led to further studies on the notion of binary opposition—the need of the human mind to divide everything into opposing pairs. The dynamics of politics inevitably split into the conflict of Left versus Right. Sports competitions become heated paired rivalries. The angst of urban poverty divides neighbors into opposing gangs. We create a world where one must take sides. Further, a tendency exists to consider one side as privileged while its twin deficient. The hero over the villain. Light over darkness. One of the two binary oppositions is viewed as holding goodness while its opposite possesses evil. Language supports this tendency with words containing culturally influenced privileges and prejudices. Male may be discretely pictured as dominant over female. Racial white over color. According to Derrida, language supports a "violent hierarchy" of one term dominating the other.

Since Derrida's studies, the word pharmakon has often been used to mean any word carrying contradictory meanings. Examples include the words custom (meaning both common and unique), buckle (both to secure and to collapse), overlook (both to inspect and fail to inspect) and sanction (both to approve and to penalize), as well as many more. As Derrida explored, these self-opposing words hint at a new way of language, and of perceiving reality. Both uses may be held at once. Not as simultaneously meaning two contrary things, which would shatter the word into no meaning at all. Instead, a pharmakon is a word in relationship with itself. In *Phaedrus*, Plato's uses of the word may be viewed, not as one definition excluding the other, but as a living relationship between its meanings. A reciprocity. Health and sickness existing only because of both. Each thriving in reliance on a dynamic relationship between them. The single word describes a single reality. Opposites twisting upon an axis which binds them as one.

Another pharmakon is a word whose attributes we have discussed at length: swarm. Interestingly, its definition includes both the idea of massing (attracting/dependent, as in the center-attraction of a flock) and the idea of spilling over (scattering/independent, as in wanderings from the flock). A tree is also a pharmakon, its dark moist roots pushing nutrients upward from the earth, its green lit leaves flowing energies downward from the sun. Its trunk of origin collecting inward, its widening roots and branches dispersing outward. Visible while hidden; diverging while gathering. Thriving in vital exchanges between.

Which brings us to the pharmakon we now embrace: home. We think we have the answer until we truly return home and it ignites. The dynamic fire between boundaries and openings; shelters and passages; traditions and inventions. We realize, immediately and in the bones of our being, that our return does not carry with it a new reality. There is no cure to bring, no better world from beyond. How could we have known until now? How could we possibly know, until our feet pass that homeland gate and we reenter familiar structures, of the fiery spark of two worlds? The electricity of oppositions real and alive, moving in relationship. Compassion affixed to protection, surrender to action. Each turning toward the other.

In the end, it is not what we bring home, but what home returns to us. What has been there all along. Only when returned is the quest revealed, is this book revealed, is our own falseness revealed. Its hopes and visions and pleadings for a newer world all part of the old. Self-contained, static, without exchange. Ideas without adaptability; pursuits without living connection. Each a fixed identity, exactly composed, divided from relation. Everything alone within itself.

To the extent that a life-giving world stirs, it stirs only in exchange with this one. Not a rejection of structure and linear but a passionate, powerful interplay. A living embrace between Venus and Mars. A great perplexity of turnings, though not a complexity. On the contrary, a great simplicity. An intimate closeness.

This book of words and its quest of thoughts must be discarded. There is no better world to build or find. No divine boon to win. Words, and thoughts dominated by words—our mental naming and favoring—are the tools of an objective binary world, creating margins of mutual exclusion. Any word is dangerous, for by its nature it chooses preference and declares condemnation. It denies relationship. And the more who agree, the more dangerous its proclamation.

Yet to prefer wordless over word, unity over division, is itself a distinction creating condemnation. We endlessly strengthen all we hope to heal. Instead, we long for a language of pure relation. New terms capable of honoring the eternal interplays of contradiction. A language looping in mutuality. Not a word but a living collaboration. A communication which circles, which no longer crashes into things with names and knowing.

Perhaps, a tree would hold the same name as a river system, not to integrate the terms but to celebrate their reliant bond. One branching, the other unifying, both expressing a mutual pooling-diversity. Tied to a single seed, as to a heart. Or a language of color-sounds or touch-smells, of subtle complementary vibrations. The continuous-sudden. Of self-light and connecting light. Of reciprocal grace. Words that receive as well as define.

An ambivalent language, unclear although glowing in awareness, because awareness by its nature is ambivalent. It could never arrive in a flash of understanding, for understanding is clarity and clarity is mental. Awareness arrives only as an experience beyond any understanding. Unity to be unity must encompass disunity; wholeness to be whole must include unwholeness. True clarity must know confusion. A *relationship*, a union which excludes nothing. We are drawn toward brokenness not to find fullness but to be truly completed, toward loss not to find life but to be reborn. To encompass such distinctions as part of a dark-light earth-shattering union lived in the depths of being.

The end is the center where we began, where we moved all along. Not a fixed idea. Neither a discovery nor a vision. Not a philosophy or spirituality. Nothing that claims itself. Nothing that stands severed. Nothing that needs upheld.

We look around. Why do we feel so vibrantly alive? So at home in the contrary winds?

Embrace of Two Worlds

SOMETHING WAS THERE ALL ALONG, even when we did not recognize it. How did we last amid such storms of upheaval and fear? Looking back, we see it, always there. A fierce holding to the promise. A trust in redemption. In healing of suffering. Often unawares, it nonetheless burns in our bones, is part of us, sustains us through the trials despite endless failings. If our journey reveals nothing else, let it reveal at least this: The promise is real. Genuine the strivings of soul. So tragic while so miraculous.

From our journeys, a gift is carried back. A message returned in our very being. Not a loud proclamation, but an unspeakable devotion. A nonlinear world rising which, once sensed, grows. We carry it in our bones, are carried within it. Carried into the tempest as its own opening. The veil does not part; the veil is its parting. Turbulence battering us until the mystery is revealed: turbulence is the creative and generative power we seek. The entry of a new reign. Our difficult travels in the tempest discovering passages and inviting relationships. Exposing the blindness and burden of our current mental system. Its one-sided truths deficient; its rigid time sequence dysfunctional. We cannot trust the dominant method of reality, cannot trust ourselves as a function of it. Unlivable as it circles and intensifies in crisis.

Like Hamlet: A wrenching loss of all we hold as true. A loss which jars us from sleep, which summons the journey. Be careful, it says, for we blindly trample.

As we venture outside our known lands, the terrain is rendered unclear. Ambiguous and, as such, painful. We have nothing to hold to. No words to say; no way to act. We are lost. Here we are asked not to discern anything, but to give up everything. Give up our decisions and plans, comforts and expectations, dreams and visions—our whole directional anxious world. We are to mourn and let it go, reconcile with its loss. A funeral pyre must be prepared and a grieving entered. Yet we have already realized a precious simplicity of self from its layered shell. There is less and less weight of self to protect.

Like Socrates: We accept aporia, choose not to choose in this third space. We suspend our inner mental dialogue and look outward for signs of reality revealing itself. Painful our loss of clarity, yet we are being guided past the walls of the cave to the opened goodness beyond.

At some point in our mourning, a hidden barrier gives way. Some grip releases. Our linear perceptions disappearing; our nonlinear pores opening. With grace, we allow the end of the known and enter beyond things. Enter into relations on all sides. We enter healing, not because the world is healed but because it empties and fills. We are free to need and be needed. Reality remains ambiguous yet, suddenly, it flows rather than confuses. Breaks open the fixed singular nature of meaning. Breaks open the fixed singular view of self. Breaks open everything! Everything as relation. The rejected the favored. The broken the whole. The destroyer the creator, and we, standing within such majesty, so vulnerable and vast. Contrary tides healing each other.

Like Hermes: Ambiguous, though suddenly clear. A caduceus of meaning and passage.

Our travels come to their final end. A life's journey, wonderful because hard, wanes in exhaustion. We sense the blackness of death approach—that curtain beyond which no landscape can be known, if landscape there be. Into the risk of nothingness we are tasked to allow. The culmination of our long quest calls to us, asking that we rely in death upon patterns gifted in life. In our right hand, we hold water; in our left, a sail. We enter the end, finally, as it truly is—such dignity, such trust, for it is neither death nor life, but the coupling. The fulcrum of the turnings. The heart joining dark to light, stars to sun, in ever-present embrace. How beauteous we are! All is! Spun from the same thread as dreams. Spun from the love between death and life.

While unspeakable, it is not quiet. Returning, the union overwhelms all things. Attracting, looping, amplifying. Like lightning, it breaks across the universe. Immediate and immense. Intimate and overpowering. Building to a threshold. Leaping into creation.

Awake, dear heart, awake. Some great coming stirs to life. An undying promise rises. The beginning.